SANCTIONS AND SWEETENERS

RIGHTS AND RESPONSIBILITIES IN THE BENEFITS SYSTEM

KATE STANLEY AND LIANE ASTA LOHDE
WITH STUART WHITE

The ippr

The **Institute for Public Policy Research** (ippr) is the UK's leading progressive think tank and was established in 1988. Its role is to bridge the political divide between the social democratic and liberal traditions, the intellectual divide between academia and the policy making establishment and the cultural divide between government and civil society. It is first and foremost a research institute, aiming to provide innovative and credible policy solutions. Its work, the questions its research poses and the methods it uses are driven by the belief that the journey to a good society is one that places social justice, democratic participation and economic and environmental sustainability at its core.

For further information you can contact ippr's external affairs department on info@ippr.org, you can view our website at www.ippr.org and you can buy our books from Central Books on 0845 458 9910 or email ippr@centralbooks.com.

Our trustees

© IPPR 2004
Typeset by Emphasis

with compliments

institute for public policy research
30–32 Southampton Street
London WC2E 7RA
Tel +44 (0)20 7470 6100
Fax +44 (0)20 7470 6111
Email info@ippr.org
www.ippr.org

ippr

CONTENTS

Acknowledgments

We would like to thank our project partners without whom this project would not have been possible. They are: the Chartered Institute for Housing, Castle Vale Housing Action Trust, the Disability Rights Commission, Leonard Cheshire, London and Quadrant Housing Association, the National Housing Federation and Shelter.

We would also like to thank Dr Alan Deacon and Prof Larry Mead for their contributions to the scoping seminar. Thank you also to ippr staff past and present: Lula Durante, Laura Edwards, Rachel O'Brien, Howard Reed, Sue Regan, Peter Robinson, Abigail Rowe and John Schwartz and our project interns Julia Crossfield, Nora Kovacheva and Pedram Parasmund. Julia Crossfield prepared a paper on the learning from social psychology, which helped to inform the thinking on this subject in this report. However, responsibility for this report and its contents lies with the authors alone.

The authors

Kate Stanley is a Senior Research Fellow and Head of Social Policy at the ippr. **Liane Asta Lohde** was a Research Assistant in Social Policy at the ippr.

Dr Stuart White is Tutor and Fellow at Jesus College, University of Oxford. He is author of Section 1 and the contents of the rest of the report do not necessarily reflect his views.

Executive summary

There have always been conditions imposed on the receipt of benefits but recent policy decisions have extended use of conditionality and the trend looks set to continue. The primary purpose of conditions is to influence the behaviour of claimants to achieve a broad range of policy aims including tackling poverty and promoting social inclusion. Such policies also seek to boost popular support for welfare and persuade voters that it is in their interest to fund the welfare state.

Sanctions and Sweeteners considers two primary questions:

- Are extended conditions justifiable for social democrats?

- Are extended conditions likely to change people's behaviour and improve outcomes?

In particular, it looks at the potential impact of three sets of policy proposals:

- the extension of work-related conditions on Income Support for lone parents;

- the extension of work-related conditions on Incapacity Benefit for disabled people[1]; and

- the extension of behavioural conditions on Housing Benefit to tackle anti-social behaviour.

Lone parents

Sanctions and Sweeteners concludes that the extension of work-related requirements on lone parents is compatible with social democracy, and is reasonably likely to reduce the numbers of workless households and thereby reduce child poverty.

However, such a policy would require numerous other conditions to be met to ensure that it was effective and just. These conditions include, among others: further improvement in the childcare infrastructure; substantial in-work financial support and continuing stability; and relative security in the labour market in which suitable jobs are available. Meeting these conditions would be a substantial task and the policy would need to be resource intensive to deliver in a just and effective manner. Current welfare to work policies for lone parents have already had some success. This means that – given the need to prioritise – it would not be advisable to prioritise the extension of conditions on Income Support for lone parents.

1 In this report, 'disabled people' is used as a shorthand term used here to refer to people with a long-term disability or health problem. This shorthand is also used to refer to people claiming Incapacity Benefit. However, it is recognised that there are people claiming Incapacity Benefit who do not consider themselves to be disabled.

Disabled people

Sanctions and Sweeteners concludes that work-related conditions on Incapacity Benefit for disabled people should not currently be extended. There are three central reasons for this:

- Inadequate policy foundations – the benefits structure for disabled people is unable to respond adequately to the need to support more disabled people into work and provide support to those for whom work is not an option.

- Difficulties in identifying capacity for work – it is extremely difficult to make the distinction between those for whom work is not an option at a given point in time, and those for whom some form of work is possible. This makes extended work-related conditions difficult and high risk to implement.

- Lack of evidence of what works for whom – there is a need to make welfare to work programmes more effective before making them mandatory, this includes tackling demand-side barriers, such as employer discrimination.

Rather, the report argues, there is a need to reform the incapacity benefits regime in order to resolve the central paradox at the heart of any attempt to link Incapacity Benefit and work conditions: in order to be eligible to claim Incapacity Benefit a person must demonstrate their incapacity to work, so requiring that they seek work in order to claim Incapacity Benefit seems logically absurd. Welfare to work programmes such as Pathways to Work should also be extended.

Anti-social tenants

Sanctions and Sweeteners concludes that recent proposals to extend behavioural conditions on the receipt of Housing Benefit provide an important illustration of the limitations of conditionality as a policy tool. Behaviour-based conditions should not be attached to Housing Benefit because such conditionality would not address the root causes of anti-social behaviour and therefore would not be a viable long-term solution; furthermore they would be extremely difficult to implement in a just way and they would lead to an inequitable enforcement of the duty to behave civilly because they could only be applied to people in receipt of Housing Benefit.

There are viable alternatives to such conditionality that would achieve the same objective without the attendant risks. The relevant authorities have a range of tools available to tackle anti-social behaviour and the Government should support more holistic interventions such as those being piloted in Dundee and Rotherham.

The analytic framework

The first section of *Sanctions and Sweeteners* sets up an analytic framework to assess whether a policy proposal is justifiable in social democratic terms. The framework poses three tests:

1 Does the conditionality proposal have a clear rationale in terms of social democratic values such as economic reciprocity, equality of opportunity and civility?

2 Is the claimed behavioural impact a reasonable supposition in view of the evidence to hand?

3 Is the conditionality policy, in conjunction with other relevant policies, fair in an overall sense?

If a policy passes all three tests, it can be said to be good policy.

Applying the framework

In the second section of this report, the framework is applied to assess extended conditionality in relation to the policies for lone parents, disabled people and anti-social tenants. Evidence is drawn from the US and Europe as well as from the impact of extended conditionality on other groups in the UK – and as one purpose of extended conditionality is to boost public support for welfare, public opinion is also considered.

Lone parents

1 *Rationale:* There are social democratic justifications for extending the work-related conditions on lone parents, including promoting equality of opportunity and – some would argue – on paternalistic grounds. For example, paid work can help lone parents move out of poverty and so enhance equality of opportunity for their children. It can also enhance equality of opportunity for women through economic empowerment. Test one is passed.

2 *Evidence:* In recent years, whilst conditions in the form of work-focused interviews (WFIs) have been in place, there have been improvements in the employment, income and poverty rates of lone parents. However, it is far from clear that all this improvement can be attributed to existing work requirements. Evidence shows it is the combination of WFIs with other factors and policies, including a stable economy, the voluntary New Deal for Lone Parents and tax credits, which have been important in bringing about these improvements. Test two is passed, but with significant qualifications.

3 *Unfair side effects:* Inequity in the enforcement of social duties amongst lone parents may result from inconsistent application of conditionality

rules but improvements in implementation ought to be able to make this problem tolerable. Extended work conditions also imply inequity between lone parents and parents in two-parent families where one parent works in the paid labour market and one in the unpaid domestic sphere; and between lone parents and people who have inherited wealth and are also living off unearned income but without the requirement for economic reciprocity. Again, these may be acceptable inequities if conditionality results in better outcomes for lone parents and their children – and the evidence suggests it might, provided high quality childcare was accessible and affordable. The UK is unusual amongst European Union countries in not requiring lone parents to fulfil work conditions once their children reach a certain age, and stringent work conditions are applied in the US. There seems to be cross-European evidence that where a requirement is imposed on lone parents to seek work after their children reach a certain age, more generous benefits are provided for lone parents with younger children, and in-work benefits are provided for lone parents for older children. This trade-off as well as significant infrastructural and support investment would be further necessary conditions for extended conditionality and, with these additional requirements, test three is passed.

Disabled people

1 *Rationale:* The extension of work-related conditions on the receipt of Incapacity Benefit (IB) can be justified through the social democratic rationale of promoting equality of opportunity, by seeking to enhance disabled people's chances of moving into work. Work is one route out of poverty and can enable social and economic inclusion and therefore should be promoted amongst disabled people, who have a very high rate of poverty and social exclusion. However, within the current benefits system, this rationale must be combined with paternalistic considerations if test one is to be passed. This is because there is a fundamental problem that lies at the heart of IB which acts as a powerful disincentive for people for whom work would lead to economic and social inclusion. The structure and rules of IB have been combined with welfare to work efforts to create a situation where, on the one hand people must demonstrate their incapacity for work in order to be eligible for IB, and on the other hand they are required to attend an interview to discuss how they might work. This contradiction leads to uncertainty, risk aversion and misunderstandings amongst both disabled people and their potential employers about their ability and eligibility to seek and take work. It is not possible to say that test one is clearly passed.

2 *Evidence:* The evidence is weak on what works for whom as attempts to promote the labour market participation of disabled people in the UK

have so far met with only moderate success in terms of increasing the skills and employability of disabled people (partly as a result of long-term under-investment in spending on welfare to work for disabled people). No country, in fact, appears to have a scheme capable of delivering significant positive impacts on the economic and social integration of disabled people. Implementation of work conditions would require a massive increase in the capacity of Jobcentre Plus and a substantial increase in public spending on labour market programmes for disabled people. Just extending WFIs to all existing claimants could take as long as ten years at current capacity levels. Research also shows that work-related options for disabled people need to be closely matched to individual needs to be effective, so a much wider range of programme and support services would need to be made available. On the basis of existing evidence, test two can be said to have been failed as even if extended conditions brought about behavioural change they may not lead to improved outcomes.

3   *Unfair side effects:* Most of the issues described above are practical challenges but if they were not dealt with effectively, extended conditionality would be highly likely to result in a considerable risk of harm to disabled people. For example, a failure to determine accurately who should and should not be required to undertake work-related activities could lead to people being sanctioned for failure to comply with conditions with which they are not capable of complying. Or, a failure to tackle discrimination by employers or to tackle wider barriers to work such as inaccessible transport would mean disabled people, including those with mental health problems, would be subject to potentially highly demoralising and unrealistic expectations. These risks mean that test three is failed.

Anti-social tenants

1   *Rationale:* In 2003 the Government proposed giving local authorities an enabling power to withhold payments of Housing Benefit from individual tenants where they believed this was the most effective way of tackling anti-social behaviour. This proposal can be said to be based on the social democratic value of civility and test one is passed.

2   *Evidence:* The primary argument for suggesting that the proposal would fail to reduce anti-social behaviour is that the policy would not deal with the root causes. A body of research has identified that perpetrators of anti-social behaviour often face a complex range of problems, including poverty, unemployment and drug dependency, and this proposal would do nothing to address these issues. Whilst the condition might be effective in changing behaviour, it would not be able to tackle the

underlying causes of anti-social behaviour and so is unlikely to be successful in the longer term. Test two is failed.

3   *Unfair side effects:* The policy could only be applied to people who are in receipt of Housing Benefit, probably the most class-defined benefit, and includes no means of tackling anti-social behaviour amongst people not claiming Housing Benefit so would be inequitable in its effects. There are also risks of harm to the most disadvantaged, for example it might lead to homelessness. The policy may also punish those people who cannot control their behaviour, such as those with mental health issues, or those who are not able to control visitors or family members. Or it may lead to harm to innocent third parties such as siblings or mothers. On those grounds, test three is failed.

Evidence from other groups

The impact of conditions on other benefit claimant groups can provide further evidence of the possible impacts of any extension of the conditions on the groups focused on here. The evidence of changed behaviour shows a mixed picture and some unfair side effects have been identified. While there are reasonable grounds to suppose that extended conditions can change behaviour, the case is not overwhelming and if these changes are to deliver improved outcomes then careful attention must be paid to implementation and communication.

Public opinion

Strengthening public support for the benefits system is a key motivation for the Government in extending conditions on benefits. But on the basis of the available evidence – which is limited – it is not possible to identify a clear demand from the public that extended conditions should be imposed on lone parents, disabled people or anti-social tenants, although there is clear support for a broad framework of rights and responsibilities and conditions being placed on those who are in a position to fulfil them.

Conditionality as a policy tool

Applying a social democratic framework to three specific policy proposals demonstrates the limitations of benefit conditionality and shows that it is not an appropriate tool for achieving certain outcomes. Extended conditionality can often be justified using social democratic rationale and there are grounds for thinking extended benefit conditions can bring about behavioural change. However, there is a more positive conceptualisation of rights and responsibilities than 'pure' extended conditionality implies, one in which people are supported to fulfil their responsibilities and society acknowledges its own responsibilities to disadvantaged people.

Introduction
Kate Stanley

'Rights and responsibilities' is a concept commonly used by the current Labour Government to express its approach to the British benefit system. By 'rights and responsibilities' it means that it will ensure the right to state support at times of need, so long as people fulfil their responsibilities to take the opportunities provided and to meet certain standards of behaviour. This social contract is enforced with sanctions and incentivised with sweeteners.

This report aims to inform the development of public policy in relation to the conditions placed upon benefit receipt in the welfare system. It considers two primary questions:

- Are extended conditions justifiable for social democrats?

- Do they work both by changing behaviour and thereby improving outcomes, and boosting public support for the benefit system?

It identifies the implications of this analysis for public policy and suggests some ways forward.

'Conditionality' is the principle that entitlement to benefits should be conditional on satisfying certain conditions, most commonly undertaking work-related activity such as job search. There have always been conditions imposed on the receipt of benefits but in recent years new and more conditions have been imposed on a wider range of benefits, sometimes referred to as 'extended conditionality'; for example, the New Deal for Young People with its increased work requirements, or the proposal (subsequently dropped) to sanction the removal of Housing Benefit of people repeatedly committing anti-social behaviour. The primary aim of such conditions is to influence the way people behave in order to achieve a broad range of policy aims. This extension of conditions is not, however, supported by a robust analysis of the legitimacy and justification of using the welfare system in this way. Nor is it supported by a robust analysis of the available evidence on its possible impact. This evidence is required to demonstrate if extended conditionality is an effective policy tool. Current discussion of this policy trend is taking place within an analytical vacuum and policies are being advanced with little empirical understanding of their potential consequences or impact.

An ippr scoping seminar[2] established that there was a high degree of scepticism about the value of extended conditionality but there was very little evidence on which to make an informed judgement. This report presents

2 A summary of the seminar presentations and discussion is available at: www.ippr.org/research/social policy/beyond activewelfare.

the findings of the subsequent review of the UK and international literature and discussions with a wide range of stakeholders. It aims to begin to address this gap and on this basis indicate how policy and practice in this area could be developed to achieve the best outcomes for benefit recipients, their dependents and the wider community.

This introduction sets the context by sketching out the role of conditionality in the UK welfare system and the importance of the concept of rights and responsibilities in current rhetoric and policy. The focus of the report is described and extended conditionality is defined. In section one, Dr Stuart White discusses the social democratic justifications and objections to extended conditionality and provides a framework for assessing the use of extended conditions on benefits. Section two uses this framework to assess the efficacy of extending conditions on benefits on the basis of UK and international evidence, where this is available. In particular, the impact of increased conditions on lone parents, disabled people and anti-social tenants is considered. Section three outlines the implications of this analysis for the development of progressive public policy.

Rights and responsibilities and New Labour

> Our ambition is nothing less than a change of culture among benefit claimants, employers, and public servants – with rights and responsibilities on all sides. (Department for Social Security 1998)

The principal role of the social security system designed after the Second World War was to protect individuals against the risks associated with unemployment, sickness, injury and old age. The welfare system is now used to achieve more than this. Specifically, it is required to play a key role in encouraging citizens to take up opportunities that offer protection from disadvantage, such as opportunities to work, learn and save for retirement. Many commentators have noted that this represents a shift – which began in the mid-1980s – from a 'passive' welfare state to an 'active' one (Ellison and Pierson 2003).

As the role of social security is stretched to shape society in new ways and becomes more 'active' than ever, policy is moving further in the direction of using welfare payments as a way to reinforce certain standards or behaviour in society, not as a right for those who are perceived to have a need (Deacon 2003a). This means expecting people to fulfil more or different conditions in order to receive welfare benefits, through 'extended conditionality'. The Government's discussion of conditionality is often framed in terms of 'rights and responsibilities' (see Home Office 2003; Department for Social Security 1998). In practice this can mean that if benefit claimants do not fulfil their responsibilities to behave in certain ways, such as look for a job, they forgo their rights to benefit and are sanctioned through its withdrawal, at least partially and for a period.

Of course, placing conditions on the receipt of benefits is not new in itself. Social security in the UK has always been expressed as a social contract between the state and the individual and some level of conditionality has always been in place. In 1911 a person could be disqualified from claiming unemployment insurance benefit if they had left a job voluntarily or refused a suitable job offered to them by the Employment Exchange. The architect of the modern welfare state, William Beveridge, was clear that the receipt of benefits was conditional. Under his scheme welfare rights were created by insurance-based contributions which depended on being in work (known as the contributory principle). So whilst benefits came to be seen as being given 'as of right' and the conditionality felt automatic, it was not (Lewis 2003). The erosion of the contributory principle in the intervening years has left conditionality as a central organising principle on which access to welfare is based. Recent governments, and New Labour in particular, have embraced the idea of public welfare provisions as conditional entitlements. Plant (2003) has argued that New Labour's policies reflect a desire to move back to some of Beveridge's principles, including the emphasis on reciprocity and an obligation-based view of citizenship.

What *is* new is the purpose and extent of the use of conditionality. The primary purpose of conditions now is to change the behaviour of claimants and 'to reaffirm and enforce the responsibilities and obligations of those in receipt of welfare' (Deacon 2004:2) in order to achieve a range of policy objectives including tackling poverty and social exclusion. This reflects a change of emphasis from largely structural explanations of poverty and deprivation of the 1970s and 1980s, to a more explicitly moral view of behaviour that says that people must take a degree of personal responsibility for their actions. Former Minister, John Denham MP, has elaborated New Labour's version of rights and responsibilities and the role of public policy in making them felt:

> Public policy ought to reward 'good' behaviour and punish 'bad'. People should be expected to exercise personal responsibility and be rewarded for it, but they must be given a realistic chance to do so… The left needs to regain confidence in the ability of public policy to change people's behaviour. We need to lose our fear of being 'judgemental'. (Denham 2004)

The location of responsibility for behaviour draws clear lines within the ranks of policy makers, academics and welfare service users (Dwyer 2000). The political philosopher John Rawls appeared in his highly influential book *A Theory of Justice* to leave no room for personal responsibility. He said: 'Even the willingness to make an effort, to try, and so be deserving in the ordinary sense is itself dependent upon happy family and social circumstances' (Rawls 1999[1971]:64). Others such as Richard Dworkin have been more influential recently. He has argued that people can only expect income compensation for brute bad luck, and inequalities (in income and other things) are perfectly just if they result from people's choices for which they can be held responsible. The position taken on the location of responsibility can be crucial to an assessment of whether extended conditions can be justified and are likely to be effective.

The current government takes a more Dworkinian than Rawlsian view but it is also a pragmatic view. Firstly, the Government recognises that it cannot deliver major policy outcomes alone and that the responsibility taken by the state must be replicated in responsibility taken by individuals for their lives. Secondly, behaviour-based interventions are understood to be more (cost-) effective than traditional service delivery (Halpern *et al.* 2003). And thirdly, the difficulty of the challenge of differentiating between those who don't have the opportunities and those who don't take them has led the Government to make normative judgements about what is and isn't under someone's control. Consequently, under New Labour, behaviour is seen largely as a consequence rather than a cause of social deprivation whilst social exclusion is seen as a manifestation of both structural and individual characteristics. This conceptualisation has led to measures both to level the playing the field and to activate the players in which it is the responsibility of the Government to promote work opportunities and to help people take advantage of them and it is the responsibility of those who can take them up to do so (Deacon 2003a).

There is one further dimension to the motivation for using extended conditionality – to persuade the public that welfare money is not wasted and recipients are meeting their obligations, as emphasised by Tony Blair:

> I think that matching opportunity and responsibility is the only way in the modern world to obtain consent from the public to fund the welfare state. It has to become the new deal for twenty-first century welfare. (Blair 1996, quoted in Deacon 2000)

In addition to a shift in the purpose of conditions on benefits, a break with the past is also found in the extent to which conditionality is now applied. Many charting the trends in welfare during New Labour's period in office cite the rise in the use of conditionality as key. Table 1 (opposite) reproduces the government's benefits framework based on rights and responsibilities. The table shows how people receiving Jobseeker's Allowance (JSA) are subject to a wider range of conditions than people receiving other benefits such as Income Support and Incapacity Benefit.

If there was any doubt that there has been an increase in the use of conditionality in the benefits system, a look at the 2004 Budget should end that. During his speech the Chancellor spelled out his desire to increase the level of responsibility taken by each individual to move off welfare and into work:

Table 1 The Government's framework for core rights and responsibilities

For people receiving JSA

- Assessment and delivery of benefits.

- Anti-fraud activity.

- Benefit sanctions for non-compliance.

- Requirement to be actively seeking and available for work.

- A Jobseeker's Agreement, and the JSA intervention regime – for example fortnightly attendance, thirteen-week in-depth interview.

- Mandatory universal intensive provision – minimum of thirteen weeks – when claimants reach certain threshold durations of unemployment.

- Access to a personal adviser service for the long-term unemployed.

- Training allowances where appropriate.

- Direct financial support for childcare where applicable.

For people receiving benefits other than JSA

- Assessment and delivery of benefits.

- Anti-fraud activity.

- Benefit sanctions for non-compliance.

- Requirement to participate in work-focused interviews at prescribed points in the claim, to discuss the help and support available to move back into work.

- New Deal access at any time.

- Access to a personal adviser service for all clients.

- Training allowances where appropriate.

- Direct financial support for childcare where applicable.

Source: Department for Work and Pensions 2004b

Along with extending the rights to support, the Government is also increasing the responsibilities placed on each person to take steps to improve their own chances of moving from welfare into work. Only by extending rights and responsibilities together can the welfare system be made more fair and efficient (Brown 2004:79)

New or extended benefit conditions announced in the Budget included:

- Piloting a mandatory WFI regime for some existing Incapacity Benefit claimants;

- Increasing the minimum number of job search steps required to be made by jobseekers;

- Piloting compulsory WFIs for partners of all new and existing claimants;

- Rolling out lone parent WFIs to cover all out-of-work lone parents.

The focus of this report

The conditions discussed in this report have two characteristics in common: they aim to change people's behaviour as well as the structures around them, and they apply to the receipt of welfare benefits. There are other manifestations of the rights and responsibilities agenda which are not considered here, such as those policies that do not relate directly to the conditions on the receipt of welfare benefits. For example, the policy of imposing fines and possible imprisonment on parents who fail to fulfil their responsibilities to ensure their children attend school, or the proposal to require failed asylum seekers who cannot return home to undertake community work in return for financial support. Conditions may seek to reinforce and encourage behaviour deemed to be positive (incentives, or sweeteners as they are called here) or deter behaviour deemed to be negative (sanctions). This report focuses on sanctions. In particular it examines the legitimacy and efficacy of existing conditionality policies in order to inform an assessment of whether these policies should be extended. It looks at the potential impact of three sets of policy proposals:

- The extension of work-related conditions on the receipt of Incapacity Benefit: an example of a policy that has not yet been adopted by any of the main political parties but has been under discussion in policy circles.

- The extension the work requirements on out-of-work lone parents: an example of a policy that has been adopted by the Conservative Party.

- The proposal to give local authorities the power to withhold Housing Benefit where a tenant receives two or more court orders for anti-social behaviour in three years: an example of a policy the Government has proposed (but later dropped).

This report focuses on conditionality policies as they might apply to or affect three groups: lone parents, disabled people and anti-social tenants. These groups have been selected because many of the proposed policies aim to impact on them and each group – whilst diverse – has a greater likelihood of experiencing certain disadvantages, such as poverty and worklessness.

The pragmatist's mantra of 'what works' and evidence-based policy making have, to a large extent, replaced more ideological policy arguments. This requires those seeking to influence policy to assess the efficacy of proposals.

This is why this report addresses not only the principle of extended conditionality as a tool for changing behaviour but also its actual and potential success in achieving this objective. In order to do this, the assessment of extended conditions (which have not been implemented) is based on suggestive evidence from existing conditionality policies in the UK, and overseas in cases where extended conditions have already been implemented for some time. Given that extended conditionality aims to change behaviour, this report also draws on social psychology to highlight any significant implications for policy making.

In the next section, Stuart White establishes conditionality as an open question for social democrats and goes on to set out a framework for the assessment of conditionality.

Section 1

A social democratic framework for benefit conditionality

Stuart White

Introduction: the conditionality issue

In this section I want to try to identify some guiding principles that social democrats can use to approach the issue of conditionality. As I shall explain, the case for or against conditionality in any specific case will depend in part on empirical issues, and empirical research is needed to cast light on these issues; later sections assess the existing evidence. However, facts do not evaluate themselves. Rational policy prescription requires that we clarify not only the empirical issues but also the values that we think relevant to welfare policy, and that we have some systematic way of integrating our views of the facts and our views about values into our assessment of policies. The aim of this section is to help policy makers think about how they might do this.

I proceed as follows. I start by explaining why conditionality is an open question for social democrats, not one that can be resolved by appealing to the concept of 'social rights'. I then set out some arguments for conditionality grounded in social democratic values, followed by some of the main arguments against conditionality from a social democratic point of view. Next I lay out a framework for evaluating conditionality proposals that takes into account the arguments for and against set out earlier and then briefly show how this framework might be applied by looking at welfare to work. Finally, I sum up what we have learned.

An open question for social democrats

Conditionality is an open question for social democrats. There is a tendency in some quarters to claim that welfare conditionality is inherently at odds with social democratic values. The significant role that some forms of conditionality – in particular work conditionality – have historically played in some leading social democratic societies, such as Sweden, casts immediate doubt on this claim. But it is important to see precisely why it is wrong.

In its most familiar version, the claim is that conditionality contradicts social democratic values because it is incompatible with the idea of social rights. Welfare, the argument goes, is a matter of *rights*. Rights, by their nature, are unconditional. So conditionality and rights don't go together. Since social democrats are distinguished by their view that welfare is a matter of rights, it supposedly follows that they cannot accept conditionality. Of course, political compromise may sometimes compel social democrats to go along with a degree of conditionality. But the ideal, for the social democrat, is the absence of conditionality (see King 1999; King and Wickham-Jones 1999).

However, as I have discussed at length elsewhere, there is a highly questionable sleight of hand at the core of this argument (White 2000; 2003). What, after all, do we mean by a 'social right'? According to one view, a social right is a right to be *given* certain resources by the community. But there is another understanding of what a social right is: it is a right to have *reasonable access* to certain resources. A person has reasonable access to a specific good when he/she is able to get it without making an unreasonable effort. Conditionality is clearly incompatible with social rights understood in the first sense. But it is not necessarily incompatible with social rights understood in the second sense. Imagine, for example, that I am unemployed and struggling to put bread on the table. The state intervenes by making available a job that will provide me with a generous minimum income. However, the state refuses to give me any financial help other than by means of this job. Clearly, in this situation, my receipt of a minimum income is conditional on work. Does this violate my social right to a minimum income? Well, if you understand social rights as rights to be given resources, then it does. But the state is not necessarily violating my social right understood as a right of reasonable access to resources. If I can do the job it is offering, and this job is not demeaning or unreasonably arduous, then the state's intervention has secured me reasonable access to a minimum income. My social right, in the reasonable access sense, is met.

So, as a matter of logic, there is a perfectly intelligible way of understanding the idea of social rights that is compatible with conditionality. Therefore, one simply cannot settle the controversy over conditionality merely by saying that welfare is a matter of rights.

At this point, the critics might argue that while this is true as a matter of logic, I am overlooking the fact that in the social democratic tradition, social rights are typically understood in the first of the two senses I outlined above rather than in the second: as rights to be given resources, rather than as rights of reasonable access to them. If this is so, then it would still be true to say that conditionality conflicts with a specifically social democratic understanding of social rights.

However, as a matter of intellectual history, it is actually not the case that social democrats have tended to understand social rights in the first sense to the exclusion of the second. It is perhaps true that the first sense became dominant in social democratic thinking in the 1960s through the 1980s (Deacon 2002). But if we go back to the first half of the twentieth century, or to the nineteenth century, we can find plenty of cases of social democratic thinkers propounding a conception of social rights as rights of reasonable access to resources, as opposed to rights merely to be given things (see, for example, Hobhouse 1993 [1911]). Indeed, there is a strong case for saying that, until the 1960s or thereabouts, this was if anything the pre-dominant way in which social democrats understood social rights. Even TH Marshall's famous essay on social rights (Marshall 1950), so often cited as if it were a clear call for unconditional resource entitlements, can be seen as falling into this tradition (see White 2000; 2003).

In short, the idea of social rights can be understood in different ways, and has been understood in different ways by thinkers in the social demo-cratic tradition. Welfare conditionality is not necessarily incompatible with all social democratic conceptions of social rights. We should, then, regard the justifiability of conditionality as an open question within social demo-cratic thought. Instead of appealing to overly abstract notions of social rights to settle the question, we need to look at whether and how funda-mental social democratic values can be used to make a case for and against conditionality.

Social democratic arguments for conditionality

So what might be the social democratic arguments for conditionality? Here I shall simply list and describe four sets of arguments. Each argument appeals to a value that is important to social democratic understandings of justice and the good society. The values in question imply duties or obligations, and conditionality can then be defended as a means of ensuring that people comply with these obligations.

The argument from reciprocity

There is a long-standing view within the social democratic tradition that income should be connected with productive service. As RH Tawney put it 'property is moral and healthy only when it is used as a condition, not of idleness, but of activity, and when it involves the discharge of definite personal obligations' (Tawney 1948:95). This view derives from the idea that social justice requires *economic reciprocity*: in a just economy, those who share in the social product have a duty to make a reasonable productive contribution in return (if so able). In the words of the philosopher, John Rawls: 'all citizens are to do their part in society's cooperative work' (Rawls 2001:179).

Now some welfare benefits can induce behavioural changes that make people less likely to fulfil their reciprocity-based duty to work – a 'moral hazard' effect. Appropriate conditionality rules – rules that make benefit receipt conditional upon work or work-related activity – can help to com-bat this effect and so help ensure that people receiving necessary assistance from their fellow citizens nevertheless respect their duty to make a produc-tive contribution. This is the rationale for conditionality that William Beveridge had in mind when he wrote:

[the] correlative of the state's undertaking to ensure adequate benefit for unavoidable interruption of earnings, however long, is enforcement of the citizen's obligation to seek and accept all reasonable opportunities of work [and] to co-operate in all measures designed to save him from habituation to idleness. (Beveridge 1942:58)

However, social democrats need to treat this argument for work conditionality with some care. Firstly, we need to be sure that different forms of social contribution are properly acknowledged in defining and enforcing obligations to contribute to society. It is important that we do not identify contribution too narrowly with employment. We must acknowledge the contribution of care workers, often unpaid, and ensure that this form of contribution is properly supported and rewarded. Indeed, social democrats should encourage an open discussion about what counts as productive contribution, one that takes into account the potential contributions of all members of society, including disabled people for whom employment might sometimes be a difficult option.

Secondly, there is a need to be sensitive to the wider social context in which contributions are made. If people lack adequate economic opportunities, then a policy of enforcing work norms through the welfare system could work to exacerbate unjust disadvantage. Reciprocity is an idea that cuts two ways. If it justifies placing responsibilities on citizens to make a productive contribution to society, then it also demands that those who carry these responsibilities have sufficiently good opportunities and rewards for meeting them. If government falls down on its side of the social contract, then it is not entitled to demand as much, in terms of productive contribution, from those who are disadvantaged by this. This is a critical point, to which I shall return at various points below.

The argument from equality of opportunity

Equality of opportunity is certainly one core value of social democracy. Some conditionality rules might be defended on the grounds that they will effect behavioural changes on the part of welfare recipients and/or their dependants that promote equality of opportunity. For example, rules that condition benefits for the out-of-work on training can lead individuals to develop skills they would otherwise not have developed, and this will reduce inequality in employment and earnings opportunities. Or it could be that making benefits such as Child Benefit conditional on school attendance will improve educational outcomes amongst the disadvantaged and so improve equality of opportunity.

Now in some of these cases there is an element of paternalism in the conditionality policies. Consider, for example, the Government's New Deal for Young People which conditions support for out of work youth on participation in programmes designed to enhance employability. A concern for equality of opportunity could arguably be served here simply by making these programmes *available* for the young unemployed, without *requiring* the young unemployed to take up any of these options. So, in this kind of case, the appeal to equality of opportunity must be combined with a defence of paternalism, an issue I shall return to shortly below.

That said, not all conditionality rules that serve equal opportunity purposes are similarly paternalistic. To see why, we need to go back to first principles. Clearly, it is the duty of the social democratic state to promote equality of opportunity. But is it only the duty of the state to promote this objective? A more plausible view is that the promotion of this value lies both with the state and with citizens. For example, going back to the case of schooling, the state has a duty to provide adequate educational opportunities for children, but parents also have duties to support the state in its educational efforts. And one way of ensuring that parents take this duty seriously might be to condition certain benefits, such as Child Benefit, on school attendance. The rationale for conditionality here is not paternalistic because the idea is not to change the behaviour of parents *for their own good*, but to change it so that they properly promote their children's good. It is not a question of preventing certain people (parents) from harming themselves, but of ensuring that they do not harm others (their children) by neglecting duties they have towards them (see Mill 1985 [1859]:175–176).[3]

The argument from civility

One of the most basic social virtues is civility: respecting the person of others and the integrity of the space in which they live (Home Office 2003a; Field 2003). Many of the elementary rights that people should enjoy in a just society are thoroughly devalued by extreme forms of incivility. Aside from its inherent unreasonableness there is also the risk that incivility will corrode the sentiments of social solidarity on which social democracy depends. Why support other people who do not seem able to satisfy basic standards of civilised behaviour? Promoting civility is, then, a legitimate social democratic goal. If conditionality policies can help to promote civility, then there is a case, on social democratic grounds, for the relevant conditionality policies.

The argument from paternalism

Paternalism is not simply a matter of forcing people to do things. It is a matter of forcing them to do things *because* this is for their own good. Paternalism, in this sense, undoubtedly plays a major role in contemporary thinking about welfare conditionality. One influential US proponent of conditionality, Lawrence Mead, refers to his own philosophy as the 'New Paternalism' (Mead 1992; 1997).

But is paternalism justified? In a liberal society, is it appropriate to force people to do what is in their best interests? Shouldn't people have

3 Of course, the conditionality in question here is in part paternalistic: in part the aim may be to change the behaviour of the child for her/his own good. However, paternalism in relation to children is less controversial than in relation to adults.

the freedom to follow their own judgements as to what is in their best interests? As a general matter, the answer must surely be 'yes' – people should be free to follow their own judgements about what serves their best interests. However, many contemporary liberal thinkers are willing to allow for a limited degree of paternalism (see Dworkin 1971; Rawls 1999). In some cases, paternalistic policies do not, in fact, override our own judgements as to what is best for us. Rather, they ensure that we do act on these judgements when weakness of will might otherwise cause us to act differently. An obvious example is laws requiring us to wear seat-belts when driving a car. Most people agree that wearing a seatbelt makes them safer when driving a car, and they have a fundamental desire to act on this judgement. Nevertheless, they also know that on getting into a car they might not bother to put their seatbelt on if there were not a law requiring them to do so. They support the law because it helps them to act more consistently with their own deepest judgements as to what is in their best interests. It is possible that some conditionality rules, that require welfare recipients to engage in job search and the like, can be justified on these terms: as devices for enabling the unemployed to act more consistently with their own fundamental judgements as to what is in their best interests.

Aside from momentary weakness of will, people can also suffer more long-term, pervasive discouragement or demotivation that inhibits them from acting in ways that, when pressed, they might concede are in their best interests (a point stressed by Mead (1992)). It is possible that growing up in conditions of severe disadvantage can have this sort of demotivating effect, so that people who have grown up under such conditions would tend to spurn opportunities to develop new skills and pursue new job opportunities unless required to take them. The experience of discrimination and prejudice, which many disabled people confront, might possibly have a similar demotivating effect. Where there are motivational problems of this sort, merely making training programmes and the like available to the disadvantaged might not appreciably increase equality of opportunity. A degree of paternalism may then be appropriate to help overcome the motivational obstacles that are conceivably part of the nexus of disadvantage that holds some people back, though the appropriate form of paternalistic intervention might well differ according to the specific circumstances and needs of different groups.

Social democratic arguments against conditionality

Let us now consider the social democratic arguments against welfare conditionality. For present purposes, I shall divide these into two categories: inequity arguments and vulnerability arguments[4].

4 One kind of argument that I do not consider here is what may be termed the inheritance argument. According to this argument, there are some resources which constitute a common inheritance to society, an inheritance in which each person has a more or less equal share. Payment of unconditional benefits can be justified insofar as it represents a payment approximating this share of society's common inheritance from nature or past generations. For a defence of unconditional basic income on these lines, see Van Parijs 1995. For responses to this argument see Van Donselaar 1998 and White 2003, chapter 7.

One reason why social democrats have good reason to be wary of conditionality policies is that conditionality can all too easily lead to an inequitable pattern of enforcement of social duties. Inequity in the enforcement of social duties is clearly unjust: if some citizens are being required, on pain of some sanction, to satisfy a social duty that is held by all, justice surely requires that everyone else be similarly constrained to meet this duty.

There are two distinct worries here. The first is the possibility of *inequity between welfare recipients and other citizens*. For example, consider the argument for conditionality based on the idea of economic reciprocity. It is certainly true that rules making welfare benefits conditional on work-related activity will help to make sure that people do not use welfare to escape their duties of reciprocity. But what about those people who inherit large amounts of wealth, and so can live idly without claiming welfare? They will be free to escape the duty to work. Is there not an inequity here?

The treatment of lone parents in welfare raises another possible equity issue. If lone parents receiving benefits are required to work, while parents in two-parent families are left free to stay at home, does this constitute an inequity? If we expect the lone parent to work for the same time as the working parent in a two-parent family typically does, then arguably this is inequitable. We would be expecting him or her to function both as a primary care-giver and as a full-time worker, onerous tasks that can be divided in the two-parent family.

A second concern is the possibility of *inequity amongst welfare recipients themselves*. This can arise when conditionality rules are not applied consistently amongst welfare recipients who are supposedly subject to them. In a recent work on the implementation of welfare to work in various countries, Mark Considine (2001) surveyed the officials responsible for administering these programmes. One question he asked them was whether they had ever chosen not to sanction someone they believed to be in violation of the programme's conditions out of a fear of physical reprisal. In the case of the British welfare officials, implementing the Jobseeker's Allowance rules of the mid-1990s, a large proportion – forty four per cent – replied that they had indeed at some point shied away from applying sanctions for this reason. This finding implies that the application of conditionality rules in welfare to work programmes in the mid-1990s failed a basic principle of equal treatment. The rules were applied with vigour to some welfare recipients, but not to others, and there was no morally relevant reason for this discrimination.

Arguments from vulnerability

A second family of objections to conditionality concerns the way in which conditionality can worsen the position of those most vulnerable and disadvantaged. There is a lot that can be brought under this heading, but here I shall note two of the main concerns.

Firstly, conditionality might consolidate the position of those who are most disadvantaged in the labour market. One rationale for having a welfare state at all is that, by providing access to urgently needed goods independently of the sale of labour-power, it can reduce the pressure on disadvantaged workers to scramble into poor quality (exploitative or abusive) jobs. This, in turn, is likely to create upward pressure on the wages and conditions of these jobs. However, if welfare is made rigorously conditional on looking for jobs, then this effect is undermined. Conditionality can put back the pressure on disadvantaged workers to scramble into work, and so can exert downward pressure on wages and conditions of employment. According to some analysts of welfare in capitalist societies, this is precisely the point of work-related conditionality rules: to 'recommodify' labour power in the interests of capitalist exploitation (Piven and Cloward 1993).

Secondly, there is always the danger that the sanctions applied for non-compliance with conditionality rules will not only hurt the adult welfare recipient, but are likely also to hurt her/his dependents – for the most part, children. Of course, it is quite implausible to assert as a general principle that the community cannot sanction an adult if the sanction threatens harm to a dependent child: such a principle would have the ludicrous implication, for example, that adults with dependent children could hardly ever be sent to prison, no matter how awful their crime. Nevertheless, there is a legitimate concern here. It surely ought to count against conditionality rules to some extent that they can harm the interests of 'innocent third parties'.

A framework for evaluation

I have now reviewed arguments for and against welfare conditionality. Keeping these various arguments in mind, I will now try to piece together a framework for the evaluation of conditionality proposals.

Three tests

One way of approaching the issue is to ask: can we imagine a set of tests we can apply to conditionality proposals to work out whether they are justified? I propose a framework based around three basic tests:

1   *The basic rationale test:* Firstly, we must ask whether the conditionality proposal has a clear rationale in terms of social democratic values. These values include, but are not necessarily exclusive to, those described above: economic reciprocity, equality of opportunity, and civility.

2   *The evidence test:* Secondly, the case for conditionality usually rests on some claim about how the proposed conditionality rule will alter the

behaviour of welfare recipients. Do we have good evidence to support the behavioural conjectures behind the proposed policy? Of course, really conclusive evidence may come only after the policy has been introduced (if then); but suggestive evidence may also be gleaned from the behavioural effects of other conditionality policies, including conditionality policies in other countries. The key question is whether the claimed behavioural impact is a reasonable supposition in view of the evidence to hand.

3 *The unfair side effects test:* Thirdly, we must ask whether the conditionality policy, in conjunction with other relevant policies, is fair in an overall sense. Even if the proposal has a potential justification in terms of a social democratic value, and there is evidence that it is likely to be behaviourally effective, it might nevertheless be undesirable if, in conjunction with other relevant policies, it produces significant inequity or vulnerability problems of the kinds described above.

In applying the unfair side effects test, I think there are two critical questions that we need to ask:

3a *The inequity test:* Does the conditionality rule generate objectionable inequity in the enforcement of social duties?

3b *The harm test:* Does the conditionality rule generate unacceptable harm to society's most disadvantaged group or groups?

The inequity test

Clearly, if a conditionality rule fails this test, this counts against the rule. It shows that, in one important respect, the rule creates an injustice. However, ought this to count decisively against a conditionality rule? Does this make the rule necessarily unacceptable as a policy?

The view that I take on this matter is that *if* the rule produces clear gains for members of society's most disadvantaged groups, *and* there is no politically feasible way of generating the same gains that does not produce this (or a similar) inequity, then the rule is acceptable despite the inequity it creates.

Note that the 'acceptability' of the rule does mean that it is straightforwardly *just*: the inequity it creates is an injustice, but the rule is acceptable in the sense that it is excusable in an imperfect world to put up with this injustice because of other, justice-promoting effects of the rule. We should not make too much of a virtue out of necessity in this situation. We should acknowledge the ongoing injustice, and we should remain committed to doing something about it if and when it becomes feasible to do so.

The harm test and the problem of mixed impact

The harm test, as formulated above, inserts a strong egalitarian bias into our evaluation of conditionality rules. This is because it directs our attention specifically to how a given conditionality rule affects the lot of the *most disadvantaged.*[5] A conditionality rule might produce good effects for society as a whole, and yet fail this test because it worsens the position of society's lowest socio-economic groups.

I would not say that a conditionality rule is always wrong if it worsens the position of society's lowest socio-economic groups. But for social democrats, here and now, I do think that harmful impact on these groups typically implies that a conditionality rule is both unjust *and* unacceptable.

Taking the value of reciprocity as an example, I can imagine a society in which the opportunities and rewards to work for those most disadvantaged in the labour market are so good (in absolute and relative terms) that I would not worry if the effect of enforcing the duty to make a productive contribution made the most disadvantaged a bit worse off. In this hypothetical society, I would say that the background distribution of opportunity and reward is sufficiently just as to make it fair to expect everyone 'to do their part in society's cooperative work'. However, I do not think we currently live in such a society. In our society, the background distribution of opportunity, and the reward structures for work, are still highly unfair, and, in this context, I think we should treat the harm test as something close to a decisive test for the acceptability of a conditionality rule: given the degree of background injustice, it cannot ordinarily be right to compound the injustice suffered by the most disadvantaged in our society through conditionality policies.

In applying the harm test we face a big complication. This is caused by the *problem of mixed impact*. The problem is as follows. It is perfectly conceivable that a conditionality rule might improve the average prospects of people in our society's most disadvantaged groups, but at the same time impose very severe costs on subgroups within this population. For example, imagine a conditionality rule, 'R', that reduces anti-social behaviour in low-income neighbourhoods by fifty per cent and so increases the average quality of life of people in these neighbourhoods. However, in order to achieve this, 'R' imposes heavy sanctions on a small minority of individuals within these communities. Substantial and irreparable damage is done to the lives of these individuals by these sanctions. Is it justifiable to raise the prospects of the disadvantaged on average in a way that causes so much harm to specific disadvantaged individuals?

This is a hard question to answer. Confronted with it, it is tempting to look for some kind of short-cut that gets round the whole problem. One short-cut strategy here is to say simply that: *it is never justifiable to improve the average position of the disadvantaged in a way that causes any harm to specific*

5 By 'most disadvantaged' I mean to refer to something like John Rawls's idea of the 'worst-off group' (1999: 55, 81–88). Very roughly this is the group in society that scores poorly on endowments of both wealth and marketable human capital. Rawls's discussion abstracts from issues of gender and disability, however, they clearly do have to enter into our efforts to specify who counts as 'most disadvantaged'.

individuals within the most disadvantaged class in society. However, this is not a very plausible position. After all, is any public policy that raises the average prospects of the disadvantaged immune from the accusation that it will also cause some significant 'collateral damage' to some members of this group? Given the contingencies of social life, probably not. Even a policy of simply giving poor people more money could conceivably make some people in this group worse off because of the odd behavioural response of some individuals to the rise in income. (The rise in income causes Johnny's dad to increase his beer consumption. His dad becomes an alcoholic and the family splits up, causing great emotional distress to Johnny that results in poor educational attainment.)

At the other extreme, an alternative attempt to take a short-cut round the problem of mixed impact is to say: *we shouldn't worry about the harm to the disadvantaged that result from conditionality rules because it is self-inflicted.* The idea here is that disadvantage should excite concern when it reflects forces beyond the control of the disadvantaged, but not if it reflects a lifestyle choice. If somebody suffers a substantial fall in income due to a loss of benefit following anti-social behaviour, they have only themselves to blame, and so we shouldn't get too concerned about this. However, this position is also implausible. For one thing, it is not obvious that we should have no concern for disadvantage even when this is self-inflicted (Anderson 1999). But even aside from this, the premise underlying the position is not in fact true. We can't say that all of the harm that results from conditionality-inspired benefit cuts is self-inflicted because, as noted above, some of it will fall on 'innocent third parties' such as the dependent children of welfare recipients.

So how should we approach the problem of mixed impact? There is no easy answer to this question, and I shall not venture a full answer here. However, the following two principles do seem important in approaching the problem.

1   *The impact efficiency principle:* policy should avoid unnecessary negative impact – that is, policy should minimise the negative impact for a given amount of positive impact on the disadvantaged group.

2   *The rescue principle:* conditionality rules that apply heavy sanctions to disadvantaged individuals must be accompanied by 'rescue strategies' to reintegrate them once the sanction has been seriously felt.

In practice, respect for the rescue principle will set a limit on the level of sanction applied to any individual: no individual can face the prospect of being permanently jobless, homeless, or otherwise severely deprived, even if the effect of allowing this possibility were to improve the average prospects of people in society's most disadvantaged groups.

Applying the framework to welfare to work

All this is very abstract. To clarify our framework, therefore, let us look at how we might apply it in the case of an actual conditionality policy. The form of conditionality that we are most familiar with is welfare to work, exemplified in the present Labour Government's New Deal policies. The element of conditionality varies across the various New Deal programmes. Some, such as the New Deal for Lone Parents, still embody a rather weak form of conditionality. But others, such as the New Deal for Young People, embody much stronger conditionality.

Are welfare to work programmes that embody strong forms of conditionality justifiable from a social democratic point of view? Let us apply the framework set out above. We imagine that the Government has introduced a new set of welfare to work policies and that our job is to use this framework to evaluate them. Firstly, then, we ask: do these welfare to work policies have a clear rationale in terms of social democratic values?

Two of the arguments for conditionality reviewed above are potentially relevant here. One is the argument from economic reciprocity, which would see welfare to work as a way of ensuring that the welfare system does not enable people to violate the social duty to make a productive contribution. The second is the argument from equality of opportunity, supplemented by paternalistic considerations. If one aim of welfare to work is to improve the skills and employability of otherwise disadvantaged workers, then it can be seen as promoting equality of opportunity. However, if the objective is greater equality of *opportunity*, why use *coercion* to force welfare recipients to take up training programmes and the like? To answer this question, it seems that the equal opportunity argument has to be supplemented by paternalist considerations. Justifying paternalism in this case requires further argument, but one could perhaps argue that it is justifiable in this context if the welfare to work programmes are largely targeted at individuals who are quite discouraged by a past history of deprivation, and who therefore need a coercive 'push' to get over this obstacle to enhanced opportunity. Thus, drawing on a combination of considerations – economic reciprocity, equality of opportunity and paternalism – one might plausibly argue that the welfare to work programmes in question do have a clear rationale in terms of social democratic values.

If we are satisfied that this is so, we may then turn to the evidence test. Do these programmes make a difference in the way welfare recipients behave with respect to getting jobs and/or acquiring skills? Assume that, in the case of the welfare to work programmes we are considering, the social researchers review the evidence and tell us that the programmes do indeed have these effects.

Thirdly, then, we come to the unfair side effects test. Here we must consider whether the conditionality rule in question generates any problems of inequity or harm to the disadvantaged that make the rule unacceptable, all things considered. The problem of mixed impact must feature prominently in our deliberations over this.

Consider first the inequity test. Now, welfare to work programmes enforce work with respect to the class of people who appear in the welfare system. But in a society like our own, some people who receive large inheritances are able to live comfortably without any pressing need to work or, indeed, to do anything else that could be said to meet the reciprocity-based duty to make a productive contribution. So there is an inequity here. This suggests that implementing welfare to work programmes against a background of the present system of inheritance leads to a social injustice.

However, I argued above that this need not be a decisive objection to conditionality if the rule nevertheless enhances the prospects of the disadvantaged, rather than harms them, and there is no politically feasible way of achieving this improvement that does not create this or a similar inequity.

This brings us to the harm test. Our first concern in applying this test to the welfare to work programmes must be with their average impact on the disadvantaged. As we saw above, there are ways in which welfare to work programmes could worsen the average position of people in disadvantaged groups by increasing the pressure on them to scramble into abusive or exploitative jobs. So we would need to have evidence that this effect is outweighed by positive effects of welfare to work on skills and general employability.

Secondly, even if the average impact is positive, our next concern must be with the problem of mixed impact. For the risk of mixed impact is clear. While some people may respond positively to the demands of a welfare to work programme, others might be pushed off welfare and drift into homelessness and crime. The impact efficiency principle instructs us to ensure that any such effect is as low as it can be for the gains we are getting in terms of higher skills and employment. In addition, the rescue principle instructs us to ensure that the total policy package provides 'rescue strategies' for people who may suffer in the way we have just imagined. What kind of support is given to people who are initially marginalised by the programme to move back into the mainstream? How easy is it for them to come back into the programme and use it to address the special needs they will almost certainly have?

Turning to actual policy today, then, there are three key questions.

1 Do the existing New Deal programmes have a positive average impact on the skills and employability of society's disadvantaged (one that outweighs a tendency to pressure disadvantaged workers into poor quality jobs)?

2 Do the New Deal programmes produce any such gain in a way that manages appropriately the problem of mixed impact? For instance, do

they offer 'rescue strategies' for those who might initially be marginalised by their demands?

3   Are we doing what we can, within the bounds of reasonable political feasibility, to prevent these programmes leading to the inequitable enforcement of social duties? (A close look at inheritance tax might well be one option here.)

Conclusion

I have tried in this section to set out some of the ideas that can inform a social democratic approach to benefit conditionality. There is no easy answer to the question of when conditionality is justified, and we should be wary of thinking that the issue is clear-cut, for or against. In all cases we need to ask ourselves:

- What social democratic values underpin the call for conditionality?

- What evidence is there to support a reasonable belief in the behavioural effectiveness of conditionality?

- What unfair side effects could conditionality have?

Section two makes an initial attempt to go some way towards applying the framework that I have set out here to evaluate some real-world conditionality policies, considering particularly the evidence and unfair side effects tests.

Section 2

Applying the framework

Kate Stanley and Liane Asta Lohde

Introduction

This section attempts to apply the three tests set out by Stuart White in section one to a range of policies. The three tests are listed below.

1 *The basic rationale test:* does the policy have a social democratic rationale?

2 *The evidence test:* does the evidence show the policy works or is the claimed behavioural impact a reasonable supposition in view of the evidence to hand?

3 *The unfair side effects test:* is the conditionality policy, in conjunction with other relevant policies, fair in an overall sense? Does the conditionality rule generate objectionable inequity in the enforcement of social duties? Does the conditionality rule generate unacceptable harms to society's most disadvantaged group or groups?

If a policy passes all three tests then it can be said to be good policy. The premise here is that extended conditions that are likely to improve outcomes for benefit recipients and their dependents should be implemented.

This section considers the available evidence on different conditionality policies in relation to lone parents, disabled people and anti-social tenants, and assesses the likely outcomes of extensions of conditionality policies. It draws on evidence of the impact conditionality policies have on these groups in the UK, Europe and the US, and on other groups in the UK. It also considers public opinion on extended conditionality given its importance in influencing policy options. The overarching question being asked is: what evidence is there to suggest that extending particular conditions on benefits will succeed in delivering progressive policy objectives? Firstly though, the limitations of drawing on international evidence are briefly noted.

1 Evidence from the US and Europe

The extended conditions considered here have not yet been implemented in the UK and so this report draws on evidence from overseas, primarily the US but also parts of Europe, in order to assess the efficacy of further extensions to benefit conditionality. Some of the advantages and disadvantages of such international comparisons are noted here.

The US

The US has been a world leader in the development of welfare conditionality at least over the last fifteen years and originated the concepts of 'welfare to work' and 'making work pay'. There is a wealth of high quality research data to draw on. The US is particularly compelling because significant, systemic changes have occurred in a short period.

The US has a highly differentiated welfare system because each State effectively operates its own public assistance system and can – within limits – modify federal provisions. This means each State has a distinct menu of policy tools, and the rights and responsibilities nexus that individuals face differs accordingly. One result is that there is significant policy differentiation and each State is a policy laboratory, increasing the potential for comparative research and the robust understanding of what works and what does not.

The chief limitation of the US data is that the evaluations have focused on aggregate results and the success of welfare reform tends to be measured against aggregate statistics. Evidence on a subgroup level and data on those left on benefit caseloads and those disconnected from welfare or employment are much less readily available. This imbalance can lead to over simplified conclusions being drawn about the impact of policies.

Differences in the UK's and the US' political and cultural landscape also constrain the scope of policy transfer, as do the different rationales for policy change and the differences in the welfare systems. For example, US policy has been driven by an unswerving focus on reducing benefit caseloads and championing the primacy of work and self-sufficiency, whereas the British approach has incorporated an interest in recognising that not all people can work all the time.

'Welfare' in the US is sharply differentiated from social insurance programmes and primarily understood as cash or in-kind assistance to low-income families, and the primary target group for welfare conditionality policies has been lone mothers. Welfare debates are highly racialised, with two out of three welfare recipients coming from minority ethnic groups, and ideological battlefields have been fuelled by negative public attitudes to welfare. In the UK, the target group for benefit conditions is much broader and the debate is not racialised. While these differences do limit what can be learnt from the US, they do not prohibit gleaning suggestive evidence on likely outcomes of policy, and in some aspects the UK is not that different from the US. Both are liberal welfare states and have highly means tested and targeted welfare provision. While moralism has not taken hold as much in the UK as it has in the US, it has nonetheless regained ground in recent years and has shifted the debate towards more behavioural explanations for poverty (Deacon 2003a). For example, people are said to be poor because they behave in ways that contribute to their poverty, for example, by not actively seeking work.

Europe

In Europe too there is a great degree of heterogeneity in programme design, implementation and delivery but the chief limitation is the scarcity of empirical studies on the impact of benefit conditionality. The focus of conditionality policies has generally been the unemployed, and policy makers have only recently become interested in other groups, such as disabled people. However, lone parents have been required to fulfil work-related conditions in many European countries for years, unlike in the UK.

There is also significant variation in how European countries have fared economically. Nordic and continental European countries, for example, have lower income poverty rates and higher levels of social security expenditure. Unemployment rates are also vastly different and welfare structures differ. Broadly speaking, social democratic countries, such as Sweden, focus their activation policies on enabling welfare recipients to enter employment through training and education. Liberal welfare states, like the UK, tend to apply financial incentives, or sweeteners, and sanctions, while corporatist countries like the Netherlands and Germany take an intermediate approach (Lodemel and Trickey 2001; Ochel 2004). Countries have also implemented welfare to work programmes at different times. While the UK and the Nordic countries had started efforts by the end of the 1980s, Germany has only recently begun to develop activation policies in earnest. The different timescales on which countries operate affect the availability of data and limit policy transfer.

Having said this, on a European Union (EU) level, steps have been taken to promote policy harmonisation. Activation policies have become integral to the EU's social policy development and pan-European policy blueprints such as the 1997 EU employment guidelines and the Organisation for Economic Cooperation and Development's (OECD) jobs strategy can be seen as signs of convergence towards more emphasis on obligation across Europe. The OECD has suggested that the reassessment of its jobs strategy should focus more on the 'mutual obligations' of recipients of sickness, disability and lone parent benefits as there are concerns about these groups across OECD countries. However, it also raises a note of caution, highlighting the need to balance work incentives with the need for social protection and emphasising the importance of the unfair side effects test in our analysis. These points of convergence mean there is the possibility of policy transfer and learning.

2 Lone parents

This section considers the extent to which work-related conditions should be imposed on lone parent benefits.[6] Since 30 April 2001 it has been compulsory for some lone parents claiming Income Support to attend a work-focussed interview (WFI) to discuss how they might make the transition off welfare and into work. Failure to comply with this condition can result in a benefit sanction whereby Income Support is reduced or withheld for a period. During 2004, the WFI regime is being rolled out to cover all lone parents claiming out-of-work benefits and since October 2004 producing a compulsory action plan has also formed a part of lone parents' WFIs. From October 2005 compulsory WFIs will take place every three months for lone parents with children aged fourteen or over. Participation in any further work-related activity, including entry onto the New Deal for Lone Parents (NDLP), is voluntary.

The NDLP was the first British labour market policy explicitly targeting lone parents and was rolled out as a full national programme in 1998. It targets lone parents on Income Support but is open to all lone parents not in full-time employment. NDLP mainly provides advice and information to support job search, training and after-school childcare to help lone parents off benefits and into work. It had a modest provisional budget estimate of £80 million in 2002/03 and generates a net saving to the Exchequer (HM Treasury 2004).

An extension of the current policy could mean some or all lone parents being required, not only to attend a series of WFIs and agree an action plan, but also to carry out the activities in that action plan and accept a job should they be offered one, with failure to comply resulting in benefit sanctions. This would mirror current policy for people claiming JSA. Such a policy does have support. In May 2004 the Government announced a review of the intervention and sanction regime with 'the possibility of tougher, more frequent interviews' in the New Deal programmes, although it also said benefit recipients will 'continue to experience different regimes depending on which benefit they are eligible for' (Department for Work and Pensions (DWP) 2004b). The Conservative Party included a proposal to extend work requirements to lone parents whose youngest child is eleven years or over in its 2001 manifesto and expected to include the same proposal in its next manifesto.

Test one: rationale

There are social democratic justifications for conditional welfare to work policies such as WFIs as Stuart White has argued earlier. These include ensuring economic reciprocity and promoting equality of opportunity. In the case

6 A lone parent is defined as a parent aged sixteen or over with a child aged under sixteen years or under eighteen and in full-time education.

of welfare to work policies for lone parents, the equality of opportunity rationale is primary[7] and may be thought of as consisting of two strands:

- promoting equality of opportunity for the children of lone parents by moving them out of poverty as their parent moves into paid work;

- promoting equality of opportunity for women (ninety five per cent of all lone parents claiming Income Support in February 2004 were women) to participate in the paid labour market and achieve economic empowerment.

Some background is helpful in expanding on this rationale. The number of lone parents has grown substantially in recent decades, increasing the overall economic significance of their employment rates. The proportion of women between sixteen and forty four years who were lone parents doubled from eight per cent in the late 1970s to sixteen per cent in the late 1990s. In February 2004, 821,000 lone parents were in receipt of Income Support (DWP 2004a). Whilst the (mostly part-time) employment of married and cohabiting mothers in the UK has risen dramatically over the last thirty years; the employment rate of lone mothers has actually decreased and was twenty five per cent lower than the employment rate of married mothers in 2003. The UK was almost alone in OECD countries in this difference; in Spain, for example, the opposite was true (Gregg and Harkness 2003).

The Chancellor set a target to increase the number of lone parents in work from just over forty six per cent to seventy per cent by 2010. This ambitious target would take the employment rate of lone parents to the same level as partnered mothers and is close to the proportion of lone parents who say they would like to work. This is the first time a target has been set for lone parent employment. It was partly motivated by the need to meet the Government's pledge to end child poverty within a generation and a belief that paid employment is the best route out of poverty (see, for example, DWP 2004a). Living in a lone parent family is one of the main factors associated with child poverty and almost one in four poor children live with one parent (Thurley 2003). The Chancellor (HM Treasury 2004) has argued that if the employment target were to be met, approximately 300,000 children would be lifted out of poverty. The setting of the target was also motivated by a desire to achieve full employment – a necessary but not sufficient condition for social justice – and a flexible labour market that requires a greater proportion of adults of working age to be in employment.

7 The argument from economic reciprocity is diminished because contributions should not be defined as paid work only, rather they should include the care work which lone parents undertake.

Test two: evidence

The primary evidence to consider when thinking about extending the conditions on lone parents' benefit receipt is the successes and weaknesses of current policies. Progress on the employment rates of groups experiencing disadvantage in the labour market is illustrated in Table 2.1 below, which shows that the greatest progress has been made amongst lone parents. In 2003, over fifty three per cent of lone parents were in work, compared with less than forty six per cent in 1997 (DWP 2003).

Table 2.1 **Employment rates of disadvantaged groups**

	1997	2003
All	72.7	74.9
Over 50s	64.7	70.1
Minority ethnic people	55.1	58.3
Lone parents	45.6	53.4
Disabled people	43.5	49.1
Lowest qualified	51.8	50.8

Source: DWP 2003

There have also been large improvements in the income of lone parents, whose average weekly income increased by a quarter between 1999 and 2001 (Howard 2004). The poverty rate remains high but fell from sixty two to 53.8 per cent between 1996–7 and 2000–1 (DWP 2004a).

So what role have compulsory WFIs and the NDLP had in improving the skills and employability of lone parents? WFIs do seem to have increased the take-up of the NDLP by an estimated one-quarter (Knight and Lissenburgh 2004). To the end of March 2004 eighty two per cent of those who had participated in an initial interview chose to enrol in the NDLP (DWP 2004a). Within this group, seventy per cent of those who had a WFI enrolled in NDLP (DWP 2004a). This illustrates that there was a larger movement on to NDLP by those people who chose to attend an initial NDLP interview, as opposed to those who were mandated to attend a WFI (where attendance of an initial NDLP interview is dis-cussed). The process of moving through the welfare to work stages is illustrated in Figure 2.1.

Table 2.2 illustrates the conversion rates from enrolments to jobs for those entering NDLP via a compulsory WFI.

Figure 2.1 **The process of moving from welfare to work under WFIs and NDLP**

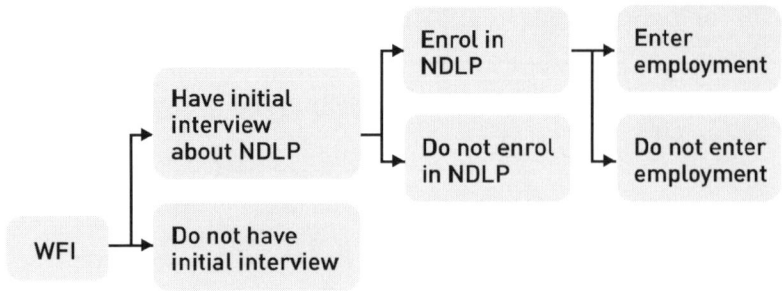

Table 2.2 **Jobs gained by lone parents through participation in WFIs and the NDLP October 1998 – March 2004**

	Total number	As % of WFI attendees
Lone parents attending WFIs	995,730	100%
Of whom, number who agreed to attend an initial NDLP interview	236,110	24%
Of whom, number who agreed to join NDLP caseload	165,830	17%
Jobs gained by those joining the NDLP caseload through this route	67,730	7%

Source: DWP 2004a

Of course, enrolment on the NDLP caseload does not mean lone parents will gain jobs. But whilst only seven per cent of those attending a WFI eventually went on to gain jobs, almost thirty per cent of those joining the NDLP did get jobs. This evidence suggests that Millar and Evans are right to argue that the NDLP 'has been a successful and cost-effective programme that significantly increased the chances of participants to enter work' (Millar and Evans 2003:xvii). Quantitative evaluation concurred that NDLP significantly increased lone parents' chances of finding work (Lessof *et al.* 2003). Importantly, this movement into work has not been confined to lone parents who already had relatively favourable characteristics, and there has been a significant improvement in the job chances of many seriously disadvantaged families (Berthoud 2003). Nonetheless, it is the case that the lone parents who remain outside employment are increasingly less well skilled and harder to help and work incentives remain weak for them (Gregg and Harkness 2003).

Most of those who gained a job following participation in the NDLP had entered the programme on an exclusively voluntary basis (DWP 2004a), again emphasising the importance of self-selection. But the fact that nearly 68,000 parents gained jobs between October 1998 and March 2004 also hints at the potential of mandated participation to move people into work who may not otherwise have done so. It is difficult to establish with any certainty how many lone parents would have moved into work, over this period of steady economic growth and stability, in the absence of WFIs. The evidence that does exist suggests WFIs have brought limited added impact. Knight and Lissenburgh found that the introduction of WFIs 'brought about no detectable change in exit rates from Income Support for eligible new or repeat claimants' (Knight and Lissenburgh 2004:12) and exits from Income Support by existing claimants increased by just one per cent. It is clear that participating in WFIs is not necessarily sufficient to move people into employment. But the combination of WFIs with other factors and policies, including the NDLP, have been important in bringing about increasing lone parent employment, as Thurley suggests:

> High levels of participation [in WFIs or NDLP] do not necessarily produce better outcomes; these are dependent on other factors such as labour market conditions, the activities on offer and the work-readiness of participants (Thurley 2003:51)

According to Gregg and Harkness (2003) there is 'powerful and straight-forward evidence' of behavioural impacts of the *combination* of policy reforms since 1998. The number of lone parents in receipt of Income Support sharply declined and their employment rate rose from the mid-1990s but the rate of increase in the employment rate more than doubled after 1998. This can be attributed in part to a more substantial package of in-work support for lone parents which had a marked effect on employment, in spite of increased levels of support for lone parents who chose to stay at home. Whereas, in the US, in-work benefits were introduced with the primary objective of welfare caseload reduction, in the UK the dominant policy aim has been to raise incomes for lone parents both in and out of work (Gregg and Harkness 2003).

Labour's tax credits encourage lone parents to work more and the Institute for Fiscal Studies has found that the working families tax credit had a positive effect on lone mothers' labour supply of 4.6 per cent (Brewer *et al.* 2002) although the lack of controls for administrative changes such as the introduction of WFIs mean it is difficult to say the employment effect was solely due to the fiscal change. Tax credits have been a major development with considerable power to affect the labour market behaviour of lone parents (Knight and Lissenburgh 2004). Tax credits are to be extended, and from April 2005 the childcare tax credit will be available for a wider range of provision and employers will be incentivised to help with employees' childcare costs. Since October 2004, lone parents will receive a new job grant of £250 and a four-week extension of Housing Benefit when they move into work. In addition, the creation of a national childcare strategy and a £20 million package of extra childcare help has contributed to the increase in lone parents in work (Thurley 2003). There is also clear evidence that improvements to skills and obtaining child support payments also boosted the return to work chances for lone parents (DWP 2004c). The same longitudinal evidence has found that positive child welfare measures were associated with working families and no negative outcomes were associated with parents working. Changes in the characteristics, attitudes and aspirations of lone parents also appear to have played a role in their increasing employment and income but these changes do not mean that lone parents are willing, or able, to engage in the labour market regardless of personal circumstances and situation (Miller and Evans 2003).

It is important to note that all these evaluations have taken place against a backdrop of rising employment and a benign macroeconomic climate, and the controls for such macroeconomic factors in these evaluations tend to be weak. As a result it is difficult to say whether policies such as the NDLP or tax credits would continue to be effective in a recession. Nonetheless these policies do appear to have had an overall positive impact on the employment rates of lone parents but it is important to ask if this outweighs any tendency there might be to pressure disadvantaged workers into poor quality jobs. There is little evidence on the kinds of jobs that lone parents have been moving into, but the available evidence suggests positive income effects from employment. Research across seven European countries found that there is a strong positive effect of mothers' labour market participation on families' income situation in almost all countries and family types. However, a substantial part of this effect is caused by the fact that mothers in employment are a positively selected group, suggesting continuing policy measures to expand mothers' labour market participation further are likely to become less efficient (Buchel *et al.* 2003).

So does this evidence make the case that compulsion should be further extended in relation to work requirements on lone parents in order to improve their employment rates and test two is passed? The case is far from overwhelming. The NDLP and WFIs appear to have had some impact on the employability of lone parents, including some more disadvantaged lone parents. However, it is extremely difficult to disentangle the effects of welfare to work in general, and conditionality in particular, from the impact that has been brought about by other factors such as a stable economy, tax credits and the childcare strategy. The impacts described are likely to have been the consequence of the combination of factors and policies.

There are also some cautionary issues raised by the evidence. Making participation in the NDLP compulsory would lead to higher caseloads, which Jobcentre Plus would struggle to deal with, partly because Jobcentre Plus itself will only be fully rolled out across the UK in 2006. It would also lead to less motivated participants requiring higher levels of input to generate positive outcomes but it is not clear it would lead to higher employment outcomes. The evaluations of the NDLP and WFIs have shown that much of their success has rested on the relationship between the personal adviser and the participant, and pushing work too soon or too hard is not helpful and risks losing the trust and confidence that underpins successful personal adviser interventions (Evans 2001). A final reason that is often put by lone parent organisations for not extending conditionality is that parents may be delaying work for valid reasons based on their understanding of what is best for their children. Given that almost half of the lone parents claiming Income Support in 2004 had a child aged under five years it seems quite possible that this is the case (DWP 2004a).

On the basis of the available evidence, test two can only be said to have been passed, in that conditionality is believed to have been one contributory factor amongst many in helping move lone parents off benefits and into work in the UK. However, in the UK it is not clear that extending conditionality would enhance outcomes because of practical barriers such as Jobcentre Plus capacity and the skills levels of out-of-work parents, so test one is passed but with reservations.

Test three: unfair side effects

The next question to consider is if any unfair side effects have or can be managed so they are acceptable in order to gain benefits from extended conditionality. Two issues have emerged from the UK evidence. The first is inequity arises from variation in the application of the rules. Where clients fail to attend a WFI appointment, they are given a second interview opportunity. Failure to attend this appointment results in a home visit by a personal adviser and a sanction can only be applied following this home visit. The sanction is lifted if a client subsequently participates in the WFI. The evidence shows that personal advisers have been reluctant to carry out home visits for reasons of security and because they do not wish to become associated with the sanctioning role. This raises questions about the effectiveness of the mandating process and the potential for variation in the application of the rules between different Jobcentres and personal advisers. This implies inequity in the enforcement of social duties amongst lone parents but improvements in implementation ought to be able to reduce this problem to acceptable levels.

The second issue is inequity in the expectations of lone parents compared with parents in two-parent families (or people not in paid work who have inherited wealth so are also living off unearned income). There is an argument that imposing conditionality on lone parents devalues childcare by prioritising lone parents' role as workers over their role as carers. Dwyer has argued that if lone parents are required to seek work as a condition of benefit this makes it clear that 'the contribution that they make as informal carers outside [the paid labour market] is an inadequate basis on which to make a claim for public support' (Dwyer 2004:25). This highlights the tension lone parents experience between expectations that they enter employment but also take responsibility for their children's care and behaviour. The current infrastructure does not allow them to reconcile this tension as effectively as many would wish (see Thurley 2003). Strengthening the infrastructure, for example by extending the availability of affordable, high quality childcare, would enable lone parents to ease this tension and fulfil their dual roles as carers and workers. In the absence of such a comprehensive support infrastructure, any extension of the work-related conditions on lone parents could be considered to give over-prominence to the value of paid work versus informal care work. This implies inequity in the enforcement of social duties between lone parents and parents in two-parent families where one parent works in the paid labour market and one in the unpaid domestic sphere, but this may be an acceptable inequity if it results in better outcomes for lone parents and their children, and the evidence suggests it might. This side effect may be mitigated to an acceptable level by the development of a more supportive infrastructure.

Whilst some people will have moved into work as a result of the regime, others have failed to comply with its requirements and been sanctioned. In the seven months from 30 April 2001, 887 claimants had Income Support disallowed or sanctioned as a result of the compulsory WFI regime (*Hansard* 08/01 2002). There is, however, a lack of evidence about the impact of the sanctions on sanctioned clients.

On the basis of this evidence, test three would be failed if extended conditions were applied to lone parents in the short term. If the goal of policy makers is to promote both employment and equality of opportunity, there is a need to do far more than impose greater conditions. However, if the wider support infrastructure was developed, the harmful side effects and inequities might be minimised to an acceptable level given the potential benefits.

The US

Before assessing the evidence from the US on extended conditions for lone parents, it is useful to briefly outline the main characteristics of the primary US benefit policies for lone parents. The 1996 Personal Responsibility and

Work Opportunity Reconciliation Act (PRWORA) changed the building blocks of the American social assistance system, including the core programme of cash assistance for low-income families, aid to families with dependent children (AFDC), which was replaced by temporary assistance for needy families (TANF). The most important change was the abolition of 'work ready' individuals' entitlement to cash assistance. Welfare receipt became conditional on meeting work requirements, non-compliance was to result in sanctions and access to federal cash assistance was limited to sixty months over a person's lifetime. Through these measures public assistance to low-income families became explicitly tied to meeting behavioural rules, as explained by Rector:

> Welfare reform shifted the focus from material to behavioural poverty. Dependency and single parenthood per se were seen as harmful to well-being of children, and the ethos within a family came to be regarded as more critical than its material living conditions in determining personal and social outcomes. To the extent that material poverty remained a concern, reformers felt it could be best addressed by dealing with the underlying behavioural problems that were its root cause. (Rector 2001:265)

The objective of TANF was to create an incentive structure that would engage low-income individuals in employment and encourage them to avoid non-marital pregnancy. TANF is based on block grants to individual States, to whom public support is devolved so long as specified federal mandates are met. Federal mandates include work requirements, diversion from benefits, sanctions, and time limits as described below.

Key elements of TANF (adapted from Blank 2002)

Diversion from benefits
States can deny assistance to those deemed 'work ready' or divert them away from TANF by requiring them to fulfil certain work search conditions before they can even apply for it. States may also offer individuals a one-off lump sum cash payment in exchange for a period of ineligibility for TANF. This may help prevent people using up their time limits but also means that people do not receive the benefit of welfare to work programmes as they are disengaged from the welfare system.

Welfare to work programmes
Federal law requires that in each State at least fifty per cent of TANF recipients must be engaged in some sort of work-related activity, such as

---

work preparation, job search, education or skills development. Some States, like Wisconsin and Kansas, tend to exceed the federally set minimum of fifty per cent (seventy-four and seventy-seven per cent, respectively in 2000–1). The fifty per cent or less not engaged in welfare to work programmes are likely to be those who are not considered work ready. Work readiness is determined by assessing skill levels, previous work history and employability.

Sanctions

Sanctions lead to the full or partial loss of benefit by individuals who fail to comply with welfare to work requirements. One hundred per cent of benefits may be lost and sanctions do not necessarily just apply to the benefit for which the individual has failed to meet the terms. This means that an individual's failure to meet the work requirements of TANF can lead to the loss of benefits by the entire household. Sanctions can lead to the permanent or temporary termination of benefits depending on the state.

Time limits

Individuals have a sixty month time limit on access to TANF over their lifetime. States have discretion to reduce the time limit or fund welfare for longer.

Earnings disregards and work support subsidies

Earnings disregards have become more generous across most States to sharpen work incentives. Expenditure is higher on work support subsidies, such as childcare and transportation assistance, than on cash assistance. States set their own benefit levels at, or over, a federally set minimum.

US evidence is frequently cited to show how successful extended conditionality can be, so it is important to recognise that it was motivated by rationale that would not be justifiable for social democrats. The political, economic and social forces that motivated welfare reform in the US were manifold (see Weaver 2000) but to summarise, the changes in the rights and responsibilities of welfare recipients were partly the result of fast-rising caseloads fuelling public perceptions of a growing class of dependent and irresponsible individuals supported by a government that was spending increasing sums of money. Lone parent benefits were criticised for promoting a culture of dependency because of weak work incentives. As Haskins and Primus point out, the alleviation of poverty was rarely articulated as an explicit motivation for restructuring the welfare system despite soaring poverty levels from the end of the 1970s:

Many conservatives think welfare reform would be a great success if every poor person in the nation had exactly as much money after as before welfare reform on the single condition that after reform the poor earned most of their own money rather than getting it from taxpayers through government transfers. (Haskins and Primus 2001:121)

However, there was a further moralistic motivation that did relate to poverty – this was concern about the effects of lone parenthood on child poverty and child outcomes. Conservatives, in particular, tended to emphasise the role they believed lone parenthood and teenage pregnancy played in promoting the growth and persistence of the 'underclass' and fuelling criminal and delinquent behaviour (Murray 1984). There was a feeling that the welfare system enabled, if not promoted, lone parenthood, gave the wrong incentives around marriage, and at least tolerated teenage pregnancy. So further to reducing caseloads and increasing the employment rate, an objective of welfare reform was to change the reproductive behaviour of welfare recipients and promote marriage and two-parent families. So while welfare policy for low-income families and lone parents has varied by State, the overall discourse around welfare to work was shaped by a focus on eradicating welfare dependency and policy has had a strong focus on punitive measures and compulsion. These were clearly not social democratic rationale and would not pass the tests being applied here to UK policy proposals.

The evidence on the impact of welfare reform on lone parents in terms of jobs and outcomes is, however, striking. Measured against the objective of reducing caseloads, welfare reform and extended conditions have been very successful. The number of AFDC recipients reached a peak of 14.4 million in 1994 but by 1999 this number had fallen to 6.9 million – a fifty one per cent drop (Weaver 2000). Since 2000 the overall caseload seems to have stabilised at around two million recipients of TANF. However, caseload reduction has varied significantly across States. For example, between 1993 and 1999, Wyoming reporting the most dramatic decline with a ninety one per cent drop in caseloads. New Mexico was at the other end of the scale with a fifteen per cent drop.

It is not clear though what role extended conditions have played in this caseload decline (Blank and Haskins 2001). Some studies primarily credit the economy, others attribute change mostly to the earned income tax credit (EITC); others still credit welfare reform. Welfare reform also made it more difficult for families to receive assistance, and take-up is likely to have been affected. Evidence shows that the participation of eligible families declined considerably between 1995 and 1998 from eighty four per cent to fifty six per cent (Zedlewski 2002). Even tentative conclusions are problematic because the nature of the interaction between different policies and the economy are not fully understood. Further, State specific experiences cannot be generalised to represent an overall impact because there is wide variation in how policies have been implemented. What is undisputed is that the economic boom and tight labour market in the 1990s were major factors in enabling recipients to exit from the welfare rolls and enter the labour market. The expansion of the EITC which made work pay also helped reduce welfare rolls. There is also consensus that the most prominent policy changes in the 1990s, including extended work requirements, contributed to the radical decrease in welfare recipients. It is worth noting, however, that recipients had started to leave welfare in high numbers by the end of 1994, two years before the implementation of welfare reform.

Lawrence Mead (2003a), a leading proponent of welfare conditionality, argues that the effectiveness of welfare reform is linked to the capacity of the administration to implement it. This is supported by evidence that participation rates in employment activities tend to be higher where there is the threat of sanctions and regular monitoring of compliance with programme stipulations. Mead also argues that the extent to which welfare reform has been a dominant force in caseload decline has become less ambiguous with time and is most prominent in States where an 'undiluted' or tough enforcement of work requirements has been implemented alongside generous benefits for compliant individuals. Mead argues that the more recent caseload reduction is greater than economic developments could explain, and punitive measures such as sanctions have become more important. Specifically, Mead finds more stringent sanctions – particularly the sanctioning of the entire family – are linked to lower caseloads. A study by Rector and Youssef (1999) found that States with strong work requirements and full-family sanctions have experienced much larger welfare caseload reductions than other States. However, the idea that full-family or tougher sanctions are more effective is by no means universally accepted. For one thing, full-family sanctions result in more case closures so welfare rolls inevitably fall.

Sanctions were a key part of the PRWORA package. It has been estimated that in a typical month in 1998, five per cent of the national caseload was sanctioned, corresponding to 136,000 families receiving reduced or no benefits (Bloom and Winstead 2002). Extrapolating from this data, over half a million families may have had their cases closed due to full-family sanctions in that year. Caseworkers have reported that sanctions are very effective for certain groups of recipients (such as those making fraudulent claims), but usually do not provide motivation for clients facing multiple barriers to employment (Office of the Inspector General 1999 quoted in Bloom and Winstead 2002). Of course, it is inherently difficult to assess whether sanctions 'work', and which kind work best, as we have insufficient knowledge about how people would behave in the absence of the sanction.

Time limits, unlike sanctions that directly follow non-compliance, communicate that there will be repercussions in the future of choices made today – staying on benefit now is likely to mean no recourse to aid later. By 2002, roughly 231,000 families had reached their time limit. However, given the economic expansion of the 1990s, it is likely that many people are only just beginning to reach their maximum thresholds. Time limits, like sanctions, vary across States and interact with other policies, making it difficult to disentangle their impact on behaviour or to attribute caseload decline unambiguously to this policy. But the fact that in one survey, two out of five welfare recipients were unaware when their benefits would end, does not inspire particular confidence that time limits actively change behaviour (Urban Institute 2004). What research exists seems to suggest that time limits may have some, albeit limited, impact on behaviour but the magnitude of any effect is not clear (Bloom *et al.* 2002). Some States have experienced caseload reductions despite a reasonably relaxed implementation of time limits. Other research suggests that time limits introduce a sense of urgency for welfare staff, and current population survey data estimated that time limits may have contributed to caseload decline by sixteen to eighteen per cent (Pavetti and Bloom 2001). There must be a very real concern though that time limits are not a viable strategy in the face of a major recession or other negative shock to the market. If there are no jobs available and people's time limits expire, people could quickly face destitution. This risk – whilst so far untested – does bring into question the benefit that may have been derived from time limits.

Caseload decline will have played an important role in reducing public hostility to the welfare system and so is a valid measure of success; but success should not be measured solely against caseload decline. It is also crucial to look at the role of extended conditions in improving lone parents' employability and skills. The labour market participation of lone parents rose dramatically from the mid-1990s. In 1995, thirty five per cent of lone parents with a child aged three or younger were employed. By 2001, this figure had risen to seventy four per cent, higher than the employment rate for single women without children. The data shows that the increase was driven mainly by rising labour market participation among low-income women. Of women who had received welfare the year before, the proportion in employment had risen from thirty per cent in 1989 to fifty seven per cent by 2000 (Blank 2002). Low-income Americans benefited greatly from the jobs created by economic expansion in the 1990s, evidenced by increased employment rates, hours of work and wage gains (Zilliak 2003). Labour markets were tight, absorbing increasingly less skilled workers into a growing low-wage labour force, and acted favourably on wage opportunities (Andersson *et al.* 2004). The rise in low incomes has been mostly due to earnings as they replaced benefit receipt (whose real value fell). Welfare to work programmes, complemented by policies that make work pay and the strength of the economy, played an important role and helped welfare recipients make the transition into employment.

So there have been substantial increases in employment and wage opportunities for lone parents which can, at least in some part, be attributed to welfare conditionality but do these benefits outweigh any pressure pushing lone parents into poor jobs? Two comprehensive reviews of welfare to work strategies (Hamilton 2002; Greenberg et al. 2004) showed that programmes that focus on moving welfare recipients directly into the labour market have proven more effective in increasing employment and earnings than those intended to increase skills first. However, the welfare to work programmes that emerged as most effective overall combined an employment focus with education and training. Greenberg et al. (2004) showed that human capital-focused programmes with voluntary participation produced better results than those with mandatory participation.

Training while employed seemed to enhance the probability of a person staying in a job and progressing. This is supported by the OECD (2004) which found that employee training has a clear impact on wage growth not only in the case of young or highly educated employees but also in the case of more mature and/or less well educated workers, so training plays an important role in enhancing employment security. Skill development can lead to higher quality jobs which offer greater job stability and the potential for advancement and associated wage progression in the long term. Jobs in industries with a high concentration of low-wage employment are least likely to offer stability and any significant wage progression (Andersson et al. 2004). Generally, welfare leavers move into jobs in the service sector and clerical jobs, which are characterised by high turnover and whose low-wage segment has been steadily growing in the last decade (Urban Institute 2002; Andersson et al. 2004). High job instability also stunts wage progression. Work-first programmes that channel lone mothers into the low-wage labour market may be effective in raising earnings and even boost confidence in the short term (London et al. 2004) but in the long term the prospects of promoting self-sufficiency are likely to be less certain because of low quality jobs. Recent evidence shows that economic decline has negative effects on employment among welfare leavers, which fell from fifty per cent in 1999 to forty-two per cent in 2002 (Loprest 2003).

The evidence reveals that welfare reform in the US, which included a tough conditionality and sanctioning regime, was a significant factor in caseload decline and increased employment – and to a lesser extent, in skilling up – of lone parents. However, it would be a huge over-simplification of the evidence to conclude that extended conditionality was the key to these changes. Certainly though, the evidence does suggest it had a role to play and can be effective in delivering increased employment.

If this evidence is to be used in considering the case for extended conditionality in the UK, any unfair side effects must also be considered.

8 Poverty is defined using the federal poverty level – an absolute measure set at approximately $14,600 for a family of three in 2001.

Absolute poverty[8] among lone parent households fell from 38.7 per cent in 1997 to 28.8 per cent in 2002, but 57.3 per cent still lived in 'near poverty' (defined as income below twenty per cent of the federal poverty line). Lone parent families where the mother was never married were most likely to be poor and remain poor for a considerable time. Figure 2.2 shows the decline in the child poverty rate between 1989 and 2002. The decline in poverty has not been as large as the declines in welfare usage or as favourable as economic conditions may have predicted.

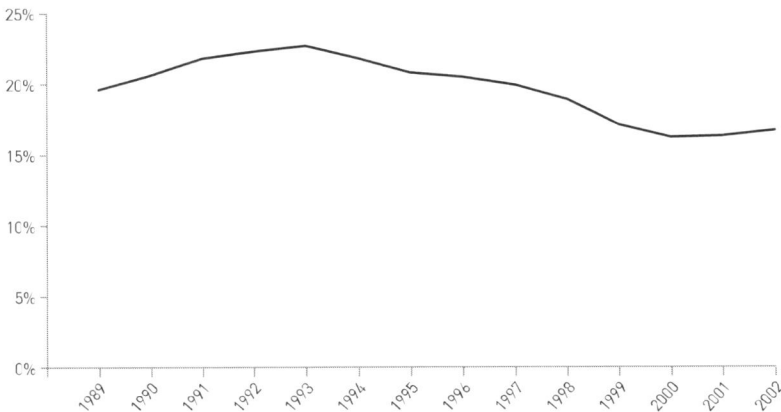

Figure 2.2 **US child poverty rates 1989–2002**

Source: Annie E. Casey Foundation 2004

Further evidence suggests that, whilst some families did better after welfare reform, others did worse. Extreme poverty, defined as poverty less than fifty per cent of the federal poverty level, actually rose between 1996 and 1998 when all types of income are taken into account and despite economic growth (Zedlewski *et al.* 2002). The rise in extreme poverty has been linked to low-income families' lower take-up of welfare benefits and their departure from the welfare rolls. Researchers have suggested that extreme poverty could have declined if welfare reform had been delivered in a more family-friendly way to avoid a decrease in programme participation. As it was, diversion practices, complex eligibility rules and reluctance to seek public assistance in the new climate of welfare reform seem to have contributed to lower uptake (Zedlewski *et al.* 2002). Food hardship[9] rose amongst low-income families between 1999 and 2002, and nearly sixty per cent reported some food hardship in 2002 (Finegold and Wherry 2004). Housing hardship[10] also increased for low-income lone parents between 1997 and 2002 (Nelson 2004). In 2002, thirty five per cent of low-income lone parents experienced housing hardship. Table 2.3 shows the levels and

10 Housing hardship is defined as meaning they were not able to pay their utility bill, rent or mortgage.

11 Poverty is measured in this table by total disposable income, defined as all cash plus food stamps and the EITC, less taxes and childcare expenses.

types of economic hardship experienced by extremely poor, poor and nearly poor families in 1999[11]. It shows that over forty per cent of both those defined as poor or extremely poor experienced two or more problems with having enough food. Just under a third of the poor or extremely poor had been unable to pay rent (Zedlewski 2002). This must raise concern about rising hardship and poverty amongst already marginalised groups.

Table 2.3 **Type and extent of economic hardship experienced by extremely poor, poor and nearly poor people in 1999**

	Extremely poor (below 50% of FPL[1])	Poor (50–100% of FPL)	Nearly poor (101–150% of FPL)
Economic hardship			
Two or more food problems	42	41	32
Crowded housing	24	24	18
Housing costs exceed 50% of income	46	17	7
Unable to pay rent or utilities	30	32	29
Moved in with others	5	6	3
Without phone for a month or more	10	6	6
Without car	40	41	20
Number of hardships			
1	26	35	33
2	31	23	20
3+	30	24	13

Source: 1999 National Survey of America's Families
Note: Federal poverty level

Little research has been done to examine the impacts of welfare reform on children specifically but some findings have emerged. Research shows that work requirements for lone parents seem to be associated with positive educational outcomes among pre-schoolers but affect adolescents negatively. For example, a recent comparative study in three US cities showed that the children of recent welfare leavers were at the highest risk of emotional problems although their educational attainment did not seem to be affected (Chase-Lansdale *et al.* 2002). Children in sanctioned families have been shown to have extremely low scores on aptitude tests and are particularly prone to cognitive and behavioural difficulties. Researchers have suggested sanctions can exacerbate pre-existing difficulties. A recent qualitative study with lone mothers on welfare to work programmes identified both costs and benefits after one year of programme participation. Costs included exhaustion and stress and less time to support and supervise their children (London *et al.* 2004). However, benefits were also identified, including greater self-confidence, feelings of independence and social integration, which all might be expected to impact positively on their children.

Behind the aggregate statistics on caseloads, employment and poverty rates, the circumstances of low-income families vary significantly. Those families who leave welfare may leave permanently because they secure stable employment. Others who leave may have reached their time limits or have lost entitlement due to sanctions and may not be employed. Still others could return to welfare but do not take up cash assistance despite their eligibility. There is also a group that returns to welfare regularly, cycling between cash assistance and paid work. Another group are still claiming benefits, though some of them may be forced off welfare eventually due to a running time limit clock. How these different groups of welfare 'leavers', 'stayers', 'shunners' and 'cyclers' fare is crucial to assessing any harm caused by conditionality.

Welfare leavers who enter employment and leave welfare long-term are the minority amongst welfare recipients. One study showed that only 30 per cent of welfare leavers were steadily employed over a five-year period (Campbell *et al.* 2002). Permanent welfare leavers are more likely to have a higher level of education, fewer children and some work experience prior to entering welfare (Miller 2002). Research suggests sanctioned welfare leavers tend to face multiple barriers to employment such as mental and physical health problems and low educational attainment.

Figure 2.3 shows the results of a study in which former welfare recipients who had been subject to full family sanctions in Florida in June 2000

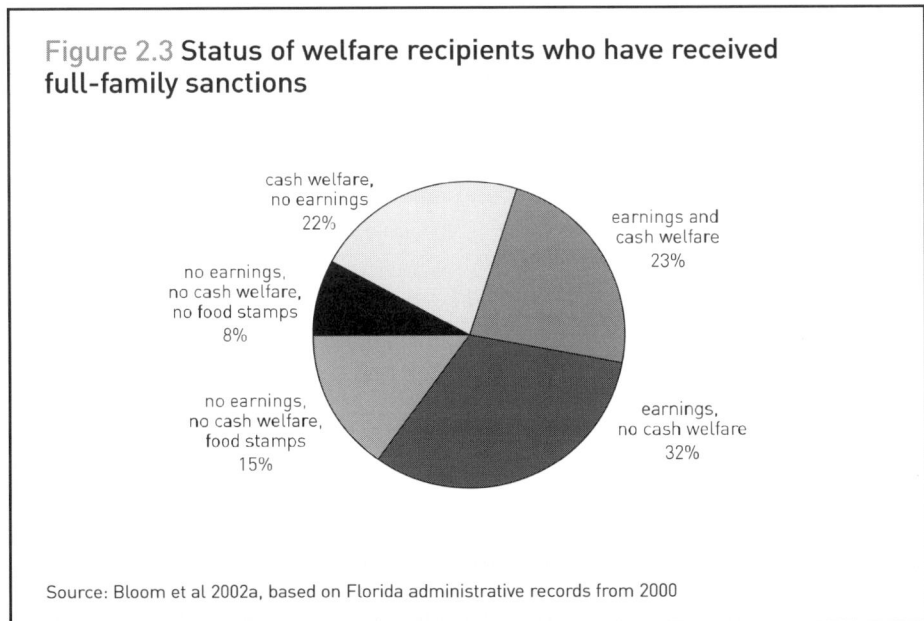

Figure 2.3 **Status of welfare recipients who have received full-family sanctions**

cash welfare, no earnings
22%

earnings and cash welfare
23%

no earnings, no cash welfare, no food stamps
8%

no earnings, no cash welfare, food stamps
15%

earnings, no cash welfare
32%

Source: Bloom et al 2002a, based on Florida administrative records from 2000

were followed for the subsequent six months. It shows that almost half of claimants received cash assistance six months after the sanction, implying that they had come into compliance. Roughly a third no longer received cash assistance but were working. The remaining group of just under a quarter did not work and no longer had access to welfare support – clearly a group of concern. However, even among those who worked and did not receive welfare in the second quarter after exit, nearly forty per cent earned less than $1,500, suggesting that they were working part-time or were unsteadily employed. This evidence appears to add weight to the idea that some sanctioned clients may face barriers to steady employment.

The proportion of welfare leavers who are disconnected from the labour market and welfare support rose between 1999 and 2002. These people often face extreme barriers to employment including mental health problems, experience of domestic violence and very low skill levels. Fifty-seven per cent face more than one barrier to work compared with working welfare leavers. As a result, the risk of hardship and poverty is high; research has shown that almost fifty per cent cut the size of meals or skip them, and sixty three per cent worry about lack of money to buy food (Zedlewski *et al.* 2003).

Despite welfare to work requirements and other sanctions and incentives to joining the labour force, a significant proportion of people have not left welfare. In 1999, welfare 'stayers', defined as those who had been receiving welfare for two or more years, made up forty seven per cent of the caseload (Zedlewski and Alderson 2001). Welfare stayers share many characteristics with disconnected welfare leavers and may be future disconnected leavers if they are subjected to time limits or sanctioned. A study of welfare recipients found that welfare stayers had a high risk of very poor mental or physical health (thirty five per cent) and less than high school education (forty four per cent) (Moffitt *et al.* 2002). The evidence suggests that this group of long-term recipients would face serious challenges in moving into complete self-sufficiency. However, time limits mean they will have to move off welfare eventually although their prospects for self-sufficiency look poor.

In 1999 almost a quarter of recipients had returned to the welfare rolls after a period off welfare (Weil 2002). Those most at risk of returning to welfare had low educational skills as well as mental and other health problems and had experienced sanctions and high job instability, had low earnings and suffered hardship. Those who had left welfare more recently have a higher rate of returning to welfare than cyclers in the years immediately following welfare reform (Loprest 2003). This suggests that with rising economic instability, lone mothers were more frequently returning to welfare. This is worrying because it means that they are using up their time limits without their prospects of moving toward self-sufficiency improving (the more they 'cycle' the less likely stable employment and higher wages become).

The increased use of diversion strategies, such as requiring proof of employment before any welfare payments are made, appears to have deterred some people from applying for benefits, which means needy people may not even make it back or onto the caseload. These are the so-called welfare 'shunners'. Lower take-up of cash assistance has been paralleled by lower take-up of food stamps and other in-kind benefits, which has also contributed to greater hardship.

On aggregate, welfare conditionality – with the help of other policies and a strong economy – has met its target of reducing welfare caseloads. However, success is not just about caseload reductions and it is clear that there is a much more complex and less straightforwardly positive story underneath. Only a minority of welfare leavers enter stable work, and those who cycle or leave welfare altogether seem to have serious forces of disadvantage acting on them. Moreover, time limits and sanctions may result in outcomes contrary to the ones intended and cause considerable experience of deprivation. If the goal of policy makers is to promote both employment and equality of opportunity, there is a need to do far more than impose greater conditions, as the US has done. Skill-building, retention, progression and wider barriers must be addressed and the availability of in-work support for low-earning families must be extended.

Europe

The extent to which work requirements on lone parents are articulated and enforced varies across the EU but the UK is unusual amongst EU countries in not requiring lone parents to fulfil work conditions once their children reach a certain age (usually around four or five years).

The Netherlands

Welfare reforms in the Netherlands in 1996 appeared to have had some success. In what was named the 'Dutch miracle', unemployment fell dramatically and employment rose. This was largely attributed to active labour market and wage-moderation policies but work-related benefit conditions were also tightened and new rules introduced (van Oorschot 2004). Lone parents are now obliged to seek suitable work when their youngest child reaches the age of five. The definition of 'suitable' work is wide, and non-compliance with conditions can result in benefit reduction or complete withdrawal. However, enforcing municipalities have considerable discretion to exempt lone mothers from these requirements.

However, research has shown that low-income mothers and caseworkers have 'rebelled' against the activation measure – so that fewer lone mothers were in work than would have been without the conditionality policy. Knijn and van Wel (2001) argue that the conditionality requirements articulate a change in the assumptions around motherhood. While previously caring responsibilities had been accepted as a full-time occupation for lone mothers, the emphasis was shifted to their employment potential. Some lone mothers objected to this ideological shift, and Knijn and van Wel suggest that the reform has not benefited lone mothers economically. In 2000 only twelve per cent of lone mothers exited from the welfare rolls as a result of increased earnings from employment. The obstacles that lone mothers face are varied but include low levels of education and skills. Their low earnings potential means they must work full time to improve their economic situation. However, these women face challenges in organising care support and weak attachment to the labour market militates against lone mothers' willingness to join it. Knijn and van Wel argue that low-skilled lone mothers have a particularly strong care ethos, which is not only fuelled by their poor work prospects but also supported by municipalities that refrain from enforcing conditionality. As a result welfare reform has apparently entrenched the detachment of less-skilled lone mothers from the labour market and their precarious financial status. Other studies of the effectiveness of activation measures conclude that success has been modest for the redeployment of more marginalised groups in the labour market, and the likelihood of unemployed people leaving welfare support has not changed drastically (van Oorschot and Abrahamson 2003).

Denmark

The Danish government's measures to bring people closer to the labour market, particularly through developing their human capital, has been dubbed 'flexicurity'. The approach combines flexibility in the form of low employment market protection and high job mobility, a generous system of unemployment benefits and active labour market programmes. So, whilst people may expect to become workless, a generous benefit system ensures they avoid poverty. The net replacement rate of benefits for a lone parent with two children with unemployment insurance is ninety six per cent (OECD 2004). The possible disincentive effect of this is addressed by mandating participation in full-time activation programmes, which also aim to ensure people are not workless for long. The compulsory measures range from work to training and education to social activities. Over time these measures have become more stringent, and sanctions can include suspension or reduction in benefits. Pregnant women, women with children aged six months or younger, and people with small children where no childcare is available are exempt from compulsory participation. The key differences with the UK are that childcare is generally accessible and lone mothers are integrated well into the labour market. To achieve this combination of policies Denmark spends five per cent of GDP on labour market programmes.

It is difficult to reach any firm conclusions about the success of greater conditionality on lone parents and their children in Europe due to the poor quality and availability of evidence of their impact. The most significant gap in the existing evaluation evidence concerns the impact of these policies on children. Poverty rates have fallen for some lone parent families in these countries, but not for all, and not always by very much. The time costs of parental employment are high, and so the quality of the alternative care is important. This may be variable, with some children probably benefiting from good quality care but others not. Older children may be receiving less parental time and supervision, which could help them towards greater independence or could mean more risk-taking behaviour (Knijn and van Wel 2001; Lewis 1997). Where extended conditions are established lone parents may not leave welfare completely and, if they do, they go into the low-wage labour market because of low skills and poor labour force detachment.

In some European countries where lone parents are expected to enter employment, an implicit contract has emerged under which more generous benefits are provided for lone parents with younger children and in-work benefits for lone parents of older children (Leira 2002). This appears to be a potentially promising way forward. The European evidence suggests that conditionality alone is insufficient to move significantly more lone parents into sustainable employment in which they and their children will be better off but that it can play a role in changing behaviour and enhancing outcomes.

3 Disabled people

Work-related conditions have begun to be added to the requirements that disabled people must fulfil in order to be eligible for benefits. A Department for Work and Pensions (DWP) Green Paper in 2002 announced the 'Pathways to Work' pilots, which started in three areas in 2003 and four areas in 2004. Under the pilots there is a framework of compulsory WFIs (every month for the first eight months of the claim) for most new Incapacity Benefit (IB)[12] claimants, although exemptions are made for people with specified medical conditions. There are sanctions for non-attendance at WFIs but they can be waived or deferred. The Pathways pilots also include:

- improved referral routes between WFIs and employment support;

- work-focused rehabilitation pilots;

- an adviser discretion fund;

- a return to work credit (of £40 a week).

Disabled people are not required to enter the New Deal for Disabled People (NDDP) and any participation in work-related activity beyond WFIs is voluntary.

From early in 2005 the Pathways approach will be extended to some people who have been on IB for over a year. The cost of extending the Pathways pilots to 10 per cent of the country would be £60 million per annum and to the whole country would be £500 million. In addition to the pilots around compulsory WFIs have been introduced for all new IB claims in all areas with Jobcentre Plus with mandatory follow up contact at least every three years.

Job Preparation Premium

The proposal examined here is extending the conditions on IB beyond WFI requirements. Disabled people do, of course, claim benefits other than IB; for example, there are many people who classify themselves as disabled claiming JSA[13] and Income Support, but the focus here is on IB. It is worth noting that the conditions on receipt of IB have already been significantly tightened since it was introduced in 1995, when it was itself a tightening of Invalidity Benefit.

12 Incapacity Benefit is the specific earnings replacement benefit based on contributions (although in more recent years this has been supplemented with an element of means testing. The wider group of benefits, incapacity benefits, include Incapacity Benefit and Income Support for sick and disabled people.

13 The conditionality within JSA can be relaxed on the grounds of disability but the provision is not used very often.

Test one: rationale

Until the creation of the New Deal for Disabled People in 1998 (rolled out nationally in 2001), no UK government had systematically endeavoured to support people on IB into paid employment. This was partly because of a culture of the low expectations of disabled people. Also prior to 1998 resources were focused on supporting unemployed people and only when unemployment had fallen far enough could resources be freed up to support other groups. Finally and importantly, it was also founded on the premise that there are some people that it is unreasonable for the state to expect to work in return for benefits.

However, this expectation of a lack of engagement with disabled people has begun to change, as evidenced by the WFI regime, the creation of the NDDP and the Pathways to Work pilots. This has been largely motivated by the dramatic increase in the number of people claiming the range of incapacity benefits. The figure has trebled since the 1970s and in February 2004 stood at over 2.7 million, but the growth in claims appears to have stabilised in the last few years and the number of people claiming IB is now declining (DWP 2004a). There are many – often competing – explanations given for the growth in incapacity benefits claims, including industrial restructuring and demographic trends. Two of the explanations of most relevance for the purposes of this report are:

- once people move onto IB they have a relatively poor chance of moving off again;

- the number of people defining themselves as disabled has increased so that there are now estimated to be 9.8 million disabled people in Britain (DRC 2004). The reasons for this are poorly understood.

Partly in response to these trends, in 2002 the Government set a target to increase the employment rate of disabled people and 'significantly reduce' the difference between their employment rate and the overall rate by 2006. Unlike the employment target for lone parents, no actual target employment rate has been set. The employment rate of disabled people rose from 43.5 per cent in 1997 to 49.1 per cent in 2003 (DWP 2003). The Prime Minister's Strategy Unit has also proposed a 'vision' for disabled people:

> By 2025, disabled people in Britain will have the same access to opportunities and choices – and hence to quality of life – as non-disabled people, and will no longer be systematically disadvantaged. (2004)

IB is designed to replace earnings for those judged incapable of work. Recently though there have been calls for IB to do more and actively to support and incentivise disabled people to move (back) into work (Stanley and Regan 2003). There have also been suggestions to extend further the work-related conditions disabled people claiming IB must meet (see for example, Work Directions 2003). These calls can be justified through social democratic rationale. Extending conditions could be justified if they increased equality of opportunity through enhancing disabled people's chances of moving into work.

Disability needs to be decoupled from incapacity. Surveys have found that well over one million disabled people would like to work and believe that they could soon, and most IB claimants expect to get back to work when they first claim but few ever do, so policies that helped people to realise this would be desirable (Stanley and Regan 2003). Evidence also seems to show that being out of work and on benefits can be detrimental to health and well-being (see DWP 2003), so it is not necessarily in disabled people's best interests to remain on benefit. Work is a route out of poverty and can enable social as well as economic inclusion and therefore should be promoted amongst disabled people who have a very high rate of poverty and social exclusion on all measures. The scale and importance of meeting this challenge is brought home by a look at the statistics. There were one and a half million people receiving IB in February 2004 and twice that number were receiving incapacity benefits as a group (DWP 2004a). Disabled people are by far the biggest group claiming out of work benefits and are more likely to have been on benefit for longer periods than all other groups. In February 2004, seventy seven per cent had been on benefits for two years or more, compared with only eight per cent of those in the unemployed group, and once a person has been claiming IB for one year the average duration of their claim is eight years (DWP 2004a). The numbers of people claiming incapacity benefits are highly regionally concentrated, with the highest rates in lagging regions, although differences are as great within regions as they are between regions. In Wales, 13.4 per cent of the working age population were claiming incapacity benefits, compared with 5.4 per cent in the South East (DWP 2004a).

There can be no doubt that the level of economic and social exclusion of disabled people is unacceptably high and that it is crucial that the benefits system works better to promote their inclusion. Within the current benefits framework, this rationale-based on equality of opportunity must be combined with paternalistic considerations if test one is to be passed. This is because there is a fundamental problem lying at the heart of IB which acts as a powerful disincentive against people (for whom work would lead to economic and social inclusion) acting in their own best interests. This fundamental problem is that eligibility for IB is based on a person being incapable of work every day that they are in receipt of the benefit. A judgement of this is made on the basis of a medical assessment which tests functional ability. However, the recognition that many disabled people in receipt of IB do want to work and believe they could has led quite appropriately to the development of WFIs and the NDDP to help enable people to realise this desire to work. This has created a situation where, on one hand a person must demonstrate his or her incapacity for work (by demonstrating impaired functional ability) in order to be eligible for IB, and on the other hand is required to attend an interview to discuss how he or she might work. This contradiction leads to uncertainty, risk aversion and misunderstandings amongst both disabled people and their potential employers about their ability and eligibility to seek and take work. In particular, people fear that if they take steps to seek work then they may trigger a review of their eligibility for IB (Work and Pensions Committee 2003).

This problem is closely related to the fact that the current system classifies people rigidly into two mutually exclusive categories: those who are available for work and those who are incapable of work. The benefit system does not allow for a gradual return to work or the need for some people to move in and out of work. This ignores the dynamic nature of disability. In the US and across Europe the same problematic dichotomy exists. The difficulty faced by policy makers is that allowing a gradual return to work would necessitate a relaxation of the distinction made between out-of-work and in-work benefits. The challenge is to find ways to reform the IB so that it can address the needs of those who want to work, as well as those for whom work is not an option.

One motivation for extending the conditionality of any benefit is to reduce fraud (and the related concern that some people claiming IB are not genuinely unable to work). Certainly this was the primary motivation for imposing conditions on benefit recipients in earlier decades. There is an argument, for example, that the tightening of the conditions on receipt of JSA in the 1980s and early 1990s contributed to the growth in IB claimants as people moved off JSA onto IB, which had no work conditions. There is certainly a case that extending the conditions on IB would act as a disincentive to new claims and potentially weed out fraudulent ones. However, an investigation into IB fraud by the DWP in 2001 found that less than half a per cent of claims were fraudulent (DWP 2001).

Extending the conditions on receipt of IB does have a social democratic justification. However, the problems implicit in the structure of IB listed above complicate this picture and mean that paternalism has to be used as a rationale if test one is to be passed.

Tests two: evidence

Whilst it is too early to be able to assess the impact of compulsory WFIs on disabled people, as data from the Pathways to Work pilots are not yet available, early feedback has been positive, with more people moving into jobs and taking up further help than in areas without the pilots. Existing evidence from other welfare to work programmes for disabled people better illuminates some of the possible benefits and risks of extending conditionality.

Attempts to date to promote the labour market participation of disabled people have so far met with only moderate success. By the end of March 2004, 79,500 people had joined the NDDP (this represents just two per cent of the eligible population) and 35,100 (44 per cent) of those participating had moved into jobs (DWP 2004).[14] Notably, four per cent of those who had a WFI joined NDDP – and whilst this is double the overall participation rate, it is still a very low proportion. The scale of participation in NDDP has been exceptionally low but half of those who have participated have got jobs, so requiring participation does have an appeal. It is not possible though to extrapolate from NDDP participants who got jobs to the wider population, as participants are a self-selecting group and likely to be closer to the labour market. Conditioning receipt of IB on participation in the NDDP or a similar programme would nonetheless contribute to exploding the myth that disabled people cannot work and change the expectations of both disabled people and Jobcentre Plus staff.

However, take-up has been so low for good reason. It should be no surprise that the main reason given by disabled people for not participating in the pilot phase of the NDDP was that they were too ill to work, and fewer than forty two per cent of those judged closer to the labour market said they felt able to work (Loumides *et al.* 2001). This may be related to people's fear of losing their benefits entitlements if they make attempts to move into work. Whilst personal advisers will try to reassure people that they are not jeopardising their benefits by participating, in reality they do not have the power to guarantee this – after all, according to IB guidelines, disabled people *are* required to be demonstrably incapable of work for every day they are claiming IB.

But it is also important to take from this the fact that motivation and engagement alone will not be sufficient to enable many to work – and many will never work regardless of interventions. It would clearly be undesirable to require people who are incapable of paid work to participate – not only would this be pointless but it would be intrusive and demoralising (Leonard Cheshire 2003).

14 Some disabled people will also still be accessing jobs through labour market programmes and interventions, such as Disability Employment Advisers, that pre-date the NDDP.

Labour market programmes have also had only a moderate impact as a result of their limited size and scope. In 2002–3, the UK spent just 0.02 per cent of gross domestic product (GDP) on labour market measures for disabled people, such as vocational rehabilitation and work programmes (OECD 2004). This is low compared with spending in other European countries, in the same year the Netherlands spent 0.57 per cent of GDP and Norway spent a substantial 2.74 per cent. Spending on labour market programmes is also low compared with the size of the disabled population. In 2000–1 the UK spent £13.3 billion on IB clients but less than half of one per cent of this (£50–60 million) was spent on labour market interventions. Partly as a result of the low level of spending on labour market programmes there is a lack of evidence about what works for whom in supporting disabled people back to work but on the basis of existing knowledge it is possible to identify three key challenges in designing labour market programmes for disabled people.

1 Disabled people are an extremely diverse group experiencing, for example, a wide range of conditions, family circumstances and work histories. Over one third of IB claimants have mental health impairments and eighteen per cent have musculo-skeletal impairments such as back pain. People both within and across these groups will require very different back to work support. Research shows that work-related options for disabled people need to be closely matched to individuals' needs to be effective. The types of services that some people require are not readily available, for example, there is very little capacity to deliver vocational rehabilitation in many parts of the country.

2 Ill health and disability are dynamic experiences that result from the interaction of a person with an impairment with their wider environment.[15] This means the capacities of disabled people will vary over time and even an individual will require different interventions at different times and may need to move in and out of work. It is extremely difficult to make the distinction between those for whom work is not an option at a given point in time, and those for whom some form of work is possible. If this dividing line is not drawn accurately people will be required to fulfil benefit conditions that they are incapable of fulfilling, or will be exempt from meeting responsibilities that they could reasonably be expected to fulfil.

3 Disabled people can face multiple barriers to work arising from both their personal characteristics and the wider environment, such as inaccessible transport and workplaces. Personal barriers may not be related to their impairment, for example, the 2002 Green Paper reported that disabled people were twice as likely as non-disabled people to have no qualifications and fifteen per cent had problems with literacy and numeracy. Over half of IB claimants are aged over fifty so may also experience age-related barriers to work. There is a limit on the ability of supply side strategies, epitomised by welfare to work and benefit conditionality, to address demand side barriers to work such as employer discrimination to which disabled people are particularly exposed. The role of anti-discrimination legislation including the proposed Disability Bill is important here. If people were to be required to participate in work-related activity, jobs would have to be available so that the rights and responsibilities circle was complete, as highlighted by Hedges and Sykes in a report for the DWP:

15 For a discussion of this interactionist model of disability see Howard 2003.

> It seems unreasonable to increase pressure on IB … recipients
> to get work without taking more steps to ensure that there is
> reasonable access to jobs for those who are fit enough to take
> them. This sounds a substantial task. (Hedges and Sykes 2001)

Focusing on incentivising and sanctioning disabled people for a failure to comply with work-related conditions implies that the problem is essentially one of motivation. There is no clear evidence that this view is well-founded, but there is evidence of employer discrimination, particularly in relation to people with mental health problems. Supply side strategies should include further and continuing efforts to tackle discrimination and making work pay, and a focus on those things that can be done to help disabled people take up employment opportunities, such as the Access to Work scheme. There is also an important role here for independent living initiatives that seek to level the playing field.

Given these three issues, any extension of compulsory participation in work–related activities would require a massive increase in the capacity of Jobcentre Plus and a substantial increase in public spending on labour market programmes for disabled people. Even extending WFIs to all existing claimants could take as long as ten years, based on the time it took to roll out WFIs to all lone parents. It would also require extensive further training as well as recruitment of personal advisers. Evaluations have shown that personal advisers frequently feel ill-equipped to deal with the needs of disabled clients and extending conditionality would place considerable additional pressure on the client/personal adviser relationship. It is clear that the skills and competencies of personal advisers are key to making the WFIs effective and lead to appropriate further activity. Current job cuts within Jobcentre Plus make the need for increased recruitment a significant challenge.

The assessment process would also require considerable improvement. At present WFIs consist of some basic mandatory questions around employment history and qualifications and a basic skills screening which does not provide a huge amount of information upon which to design a tailored set of interventions. In order that a personal adviser could enforce conditionality a specific, limited job search requirement would need to be established for each claimant. Making an assessment of what constitutes suitable work is very challenging and would have to involve people with specialist skills, including occupational therapists and medical practitioners. Even then, the nature of an impairment can change over time and external factors would play a role which make the identification of suitable and unsuitable jobs very difficult.

The personal capacity assessment (PCA), which determines eligibility for IB, is a blunt tool with which to make such subtle distinctions, particularly as it takes an explicitly medical or functional view of disability, which is unlikely to identify non-medical barriers and opportunities. Furthermore, the PCA is not able to assess the specifics of what is 'suitable' work for a given individual.[16] The nub of the challenge is making the distinction between those for whom work is not an option at a given point in time, and those for whom some form of work is possible and – for them – what work and when. If this dividing line is not drawn accurately people will be required to fulfil benefit conditions that they are incapable of fulfilling or people will not be required to undertake activities they could reasonably be expected to undertake. Two of the most significant challenges in supporting more disabled people into work are assessing the work capabilities of individuals and identifying appropriate and effective interventions. A recent pilot programme in Australia, outlined below, casts some light on ways of doing these things.

Assessment and contestability trials, Australia

The assessment and contestability trials began in Australia in 2000. One objective of the assessment trials was to test a new approach to assessing the abilities, needs and work capacity of disabled people and identify appropriate interventions to increase the social and economic participation of disabled people.

All stakeholders saw the assessment as useful and beneficial in assisting participants to meet their social and economic goals and the trials generated an increase in work-related activity for many participants. Nonetheless, of those who reached their twelve-month review during the evaluation period, three-quarters had not entered open paid employment or self-employment, perhaps serving as a reminder that even small change in the employment rate of disabled people is hard to achieve. The assessment has recently been adapted in light of this experience and further evaluation material will be valuable.

There is scant evidence that extended conditionality might actually work for disabled people within the current framework, not least because the very notion of conditions sits in contrast with the basic principles of the IB. On these grounds the evidence test is failed.

Test three: unfair side effects

Most of the issues described above are practical challenges but if they were not dealt with effectively, extended conditionality would be highly likely to result in a considerable risk of harm to disabled people. For example, a failure to determine accurately who should and should not be required to

16 The PCA provides more information on functional capabilities but still has limitations and is only available in about forty per cent of the country.

undertake work-related activities could lead to people being sanctioned for failure to comply with conditions with which they are not capable of complying. People are protected against this eventuality by human rights legislation. Article 8 of the European Convention on Human Rights provides for the right to respect for private and family life and in particular, the need to avoid imposing unnecessary and undue hardship. People who have been on IB for some time may find it particularly difficult to comply with work-related requirements because they are more likely to experience multiple disadvantage (half of those on IB for three years or more claim the higher rate of Disability Living Allowance, which is awarded to meet the costs of severe disability – although the severity of an impairment does not necessarily equate with capacity to work) and seventy per cent have been out of work for at least five years so are at some distance from the labour market. This makes it more likely that they will be sanctioned and experience hardship as a result.

IB itself is intended to identify those people for whom work is not a reasonable requirement so, in theory, no one in receipt of IB should be required to undertake work-related activities as a matter of logic. However, the IB gateway is insufficiently sophisticated and unable to make this distinction accurately. This highlights that the primary issue is improving the ability to make this distinction and so legitimising IB rather than simply adding potentially harmful conditions to it. Extending conditionality on disabled people would bring substantial financial and political risks as well as threatening real harm to disabled people. The unfair side effects test is failed and extended conditionality seems an unreasonable approach to pursue in the current context.

US

There is less evidence in relation to disabled people from the US than there is in relation to lone parents, as disabled people have traditionally been considered exempt from expectations to obtain paid work in the UK, US and Europe (Stafford 2003).

In the US, disability caseloads have risen significantly since the early 1980s. Supplemental security income (SSI) is the largest means tested cash transfer system in the US with 3.9 million people of working age receiving it in 2002 (from 1.8 million in 1980) (SSI Statistical Annual Report 2002). In 2001, federal and state spending on SSI was more than double all other welfare spending (Wittenburg and Favreault 2003). The number of recipients of the contributory disability insurance benefit (SSDI) has also risen substantially over the past two decades. The caseload grew fastest between 1990 and 2002 from three million to 5.5 million. Welfare reform in 1996 narrowed access to SSI, but it did not redraw the rights and responsibilities nexus for disabled people and work-based conditions were not introduced. A strict definition of disability based on the beneficiary's permanent inability to work has precluded the establishment of work-based conditions for benefit receipt.

The disincentives to leave SSI are powerful. The complexity and length of the disability determination process, which can take more than a year, acts as a disincentive to participants to take up employment which would endanger their benefit. Claimants also have to undergo regular re-assessments and prove their continued inability to engage in 'substantial gainful activity' or risk losing their benefit. Only seven per cent of the working age caseload engages even in part-time work (Wittenburg and Favreault 2003). Exit rates are extremely low, only one per cent of the caseload leaves SSI every year as a result of an increase in earned income, assets or recovery and very few ever leave the rolls completely. The duration of SSI dependence by claimants aged from eighteen to thirty-four has been projected as approximately twenty years on average (Rupp and Scott 1998). In 1999, ninety per cent of the caseload received Medicaid as a result of their eligibility for SSI and leaving SSI risks losing this healthcare coverage (SSI Statistical Report 2001).

Greater stringency in eligibility for other benefits has contributed to the rise in SSI rolls, and SSI has become more attractive than other benefits (Daly and Burkhauser 2003). TANF recipients have particularly strong incentives to apply for SSI in States where TANF benefits are low. The difference between TANF and SSI benefits can be as high as $400 per month even though SSI rates are themselves very low. The stipulated maximum federal SSI payment was $552 a month in 2003 – twenty five per cent below the official poverty level. One study showed that lone mothers in States where welfare reform was aggressively pursued were roughly twenty two per cent more likely to receive SSI than TANF (Schmidt and Sevak 2002).

In contrast to the UK, the rising number of disability benefit claimants has been accompanied by a substantial fall in employment rates for disabled people over the last decade. The employment rate of disabled men fell from forty four per cent in 1989 to thirty two per cent in 2001 and the rate for women fell from about thirty seven to thirty per cent. There has been much debate about the causes of declining employment, but the disjointed and contradictory system around disability benefit has been argued to be one of the most prominent drivers.

The swelling numbers of disability benefit claimants has not gone unnoticed in the political arena. A debate about the 'deserving' or 'non-deserving' is surfacing between those who see a rise in disability benefit claimants as a sign of the success of policy efforts to support disabled people and those who believe that work disincentives are too strong. Policy initiatives have been launched to help disabled people stay in the labour market at the onset of disability and promote return to work through incentives to leave disability benefit. These initiatives are in their early stages of planning and implementation, and evidence from many of the research demonstrations will not be available for some years. In 2005, the SSA will launch an early intervention demonstration project, which aims to provide disability benefit applicants with a cash stipend for one year, access to health insurance and employment services on the condition that they do not receive the benefit.

Under another initiative, claimants can work for a trial period with the continued payment of disability benefit or the security of expedited reinstatement of benefit if they become unable to work again. The Ticket to Work and Self-Sufficiency Program, launched in 1999, aims to help disability benefit recipients obtain services from governmental or vocational rehabilitation agencies or employment networks to find, enter and retain employment. A major evaluation of the programme showed that it has not been particularly effective. The participation rate is extremely low, many do not understand how the programme operates and there is evidence of 'cherry picking' among agencies that tend not to accept tickets from beneficiaries who do not seem likely to move into full-time employment quickly.

The US benefit system around disability is deeply disjointed and contradictory. In contrast to the UK where WFIs are becoming an established part of the response to the challenge of engaging more disabled claimants in work-related activity, no credible policy proposal regarding the conditioning of welfare on work has been floated. However, there seems to be some recognition, if only on State level, that disabled people need better services to support their integration into some sort of employment.

Europe

Across Europe there has been growing concern with the exclusion of disabled people from the labour market and public spending on disability benefits. Over the 1990s the proportion of GDP spent on disability benefits rose steadily across OECD countries, and in western welfare states it reached an average of one and a half per cent of GDP and outstripped spending on unemployment benefits (OECD 2003). The working-age population in the EU defining themselves as disabled reached an average of about sixteen per cent, and labour force participation amongst disabled people remained low (OECD 2003). Over the last decade, there seems to have been a convergence of policy responses with increasing emphasis being placed on activating disabled people and reintegrating them into the labour market (Lodemel and Trickey 2001). But no country seems to have found truly effective solutions. Evaluation evidence on the effectiveness of particular programmes is sparse and limited to short time horizons. Data on long-term employment effects are extremely limited, and evaluations often lack perspective on the overall policy framework.

Countries are strikingly similar in the employment rates of disabled people despite a range of policy responses that have been pursued. An assessment of disability benefit regimes across OECD countries in 2002 concluded that disabled people should be required to participate in employment, vocational rehabilitation and other integration measures as a condition of receipt of incapacity type benefits (OECD 2003). This conclusion was based on evidence that shows that active labour market policies, as implemented then, were only modestly effective, and not particularly helpful for disabled people and no country appears to have an existing scheme capable of delivering significantly positive impacts on the economic and social integration of disabled people. However, the fact that existing programmes are ineffective does not make the case for conditionality.

The Netherlands

The Netherlands stands out amongst European countries as one of the few places where notable attempts have been made to condition the access of disabled people to benefits on work requirements.

There was a significant rise in the number of claimants in the Netherlands during the 1980s and 1990s and attention focused on stimulating their labour market participation. The incentives structures around disability benefits were changed to stimulate labour market participation and access to benefits was made more difficult as the definition of 'disability' was restricted. The definition of suitable work was broadened so that disabled people had to work in jobs that may not correspond to their educational background. The insurance scheme for short-term disability benefits, or sickness pay, was also privatised, and for the majority of workers, employers are now responsible for paying their wages during sick leave.

By 1994, the Netherlands experienced an all-time low in the flow onto disability benefit receipt and an all-time high in outflow. However, by 1999 recipiency rates had increased again and benefit applications had reached their highest level ever (van Oorshot and Abrahamson 2003). Women's inflow rates doubled between 1995 and 1999. Although overall in-flow rates remain lower than they were during the 1980s as a result of stricter access and appeal criteria, out-flow rates had dropped to three per cent by 1999, even lower than in the UK, which has out-flows of roughly six per cent (OECD 2004).

The reasons for the reversal of trends in the mid to late 1990s are not clearly understood but include the end of reassessments of claimants aged under fifty which caused numbers to rise again (Bovenberg 2000). Also disabled people who had entered the labour market following the reforms in the late 1980s to mid 1990s seem to have joined the benefit rolls again. Many disabled people experience difficulty with (re)integration into the labour market despite activation measures. The privatisation of sickness benefit and introduction of premium-differentiated insurance schemes has also mitigated the potential success of activation measures by reducing the incentives of employers to hire disabled people. Equally, workers with poorer health face higher risks of being laid off. Evidence suggests that greater screening has led to a decrease in the number of job applications by disabled people leading to job interviews (van Oorshot and Abrahamson 2003).

In 2003, however, the pendulum swung again and the caseload declined for the first time in seven years. One of the key drivers for this decline was stricter gate-keeping for receipt of long-term sickness benefit. However, further reform efforts are being undertaken as challenges persist. Comprehensive reform initiatives are to be introduced in 2006. The main proposals include:

- further tightening of the disability definition to restrict the number of people deemed 'fully disabled';

- financial incentives to raise the participation of 'partially disabled' people in part-time employment;

- reassessment of the stock of existing disability benefit recipients;

- further restricting the criteria of jobs that are deemed to be 'still executable'.

Denmark

Denmark has also undergone several reforms in the last decades, making benefits more difficult to access but also encouraging social responsibility by employers to employ disabled people. Participation in activation programmes is obligatory and everybody must be active in some way, be it job training, education or sheltered employment. The long-term disability pension can only be paid when a suitable action plan has been drawn up. Studies show that the most qualified are placed into job training and the least qualified enrol in education. While employment rates have risen significantly, the effectiveness of activation measures at producing long-term employment increases are modest (van Oorschot and Abrahamson 2003). Hogelund and Pedersen (2002) argue that despite some positive effects, active labour market policies carry with them the danger of stigmatisation and incomplete integration of disabled people.

Denmark also stresses the importance of early intervention and rehabilitation. Rehabilitation benefits compensate for the costs of rehabilitation activities related to re-entering the labour market. Similarly, Finland, which has also undertaken reform of its disability benefit system, puts an emphasis on rehabilitation where, from 2004, employees at risk of disability are entitled to vocational rehabilitation to maintain work ability.

It is striking from the evidence that extended conditionality is just one method of trying to support more disabled people into work and, in fact, other approaches seem more worthy of exploration. For example, the tests have highlighted the need to reform the structure and nature of IB, to improve in-work incentives and build the evidence base about what works and for whom.

4 Anti-social tenants

In 2003 the Government published plans to condition the receipt of Housing Benefit[17] by social housing tenants on their behaviour. The White Paper 'Respect and Responsibilities: taking a stand against anti-social behaviour', declared the Government's interest in developing 'a usable and effective sanction' to address anti-social behaviour. The proposal was framed in terms of strengthening the rights and responsibilities of citizens.

> The Government strongly believes in the principle of a welfare state based on rights and responsibilities. The rights we gain from civil society – including the right to financial support when we need it – should be balanced by responsibilities to behave responsibly towards our fellow citizens. (Home Office 2003)

The proposal was to give local authorities an enabling power to withhold payments of Housing Benefit from individual tenants where they believed this was the most effective way of tackling anti-social behaviour. The White Paper defined anti-social behaviour broadly, examples ranging from 'continual shouting and screaming' to 'threats of violence and actual violence' (Home Office 2003:2). In law, anti-social behaviour is defined as: 'behaviour by a person which causes or is likely to cause harassment, alarm or distress to one or more other persons not of the same household as the person' (Crime and Disorder Act 1998: Section 1). Following significant objections during the consultation period, this proposal was dropped in 2004 but some, including MP Frank Field, are keen to revive it.

Test one: rationale

Unquestionably, anti-social behaviour has risen up the political agenda as it has risen up the public's agenda, and a real need to respond to this in policy terms has been felt. Anti-social behaviour can lead to fear and social withdrawal and undermine residents' ability or desire to exercise control over their situation in communities where it is common. A poll in 2004 found that fifty five per cent of people consider 'general anti-social behaviour' a serious concern (Populus 2004). The English House Condition Survey 2001 suggested that twenty per cent of people in 'poor' neighbourhoods and twelve per cent of people overall experience problems with neighbours. Just one example of the cost of such problems is Salford Housing Department which estimates anti-social behaviour by tenants cost it £2 million per annum (Edwards 2004).

17 In February 2004, 3.8 million people were in receipt of Housing Benefit and approximately 1.2 million recipients had dependants.

Policy tools available to tackle anti-social behaviour (adapted from Edwards 2004)

Acceptable behaviour contracts (ABCs): Voluntary written agreements between a young person who has been involved in anti-social behaviour and one or more local agencies. They typically agree that the young person will not commit certain specified acts deemed to be anti-social. They are widely used by registered social landlords and local authority housing departments. The Home Secretary announced in September 2004 that families who breach the terms of their acceptable behaviour contracts will be evicted from their homes.

Anti-social behaviour orders (ASBOs): A civil order that can be sought by the police, registered social landlords or local authorities to impose prohibitive sanctions on a person's behaviour to prevent anti-social behaviour.

Anti-social behaviour pilots: These were announced by the Home Secretary in September 2004. They will begin across England and aim to tackle 'neighbours from hell' through 'intensive parenting programmes'. No further details are known at this time.

Demoted and introductory tenancies: When tenants behave anti-socially or allow a member of their household to do so, demotion can remove the tenants right to buy and security of tenure for at least a year. Introductory tenancies are intended to be a way to monitor new tenants and ensure that those causing problems are not given a secure tenancy from which they would be more difficult to remove.

Eviction: A common tool of last resort imposed by courts where ABCs, ASBOs or injunctions fail to prevent anti-social behaviour.

Injunctions: Available for use against a tenant of a social landlord where the tenant has engaged – or threatened to engage – in behaviour that is capable of causing nuisance or annoyance to any person.

Licensing of private landlords and interim management orders: The Housing Bill includes the provision to license private landlords in areas that experience problems caused by anti-social behaviour. It also includes provisions for interim management orders to allow local authorities to take over the management of a property to protect the health, safety or welfare of persons occupying the premises or living in the vicinity.

Mediation: Mediation services may be provided by a range of local agencies. Non-judgemental discussion between parties tries to encourage the resolution of disputes and voluntary behavioural change.

Noise-related interventions: A local authority power to investigate complaints of excessive noise at night and give warning notices, prosecute or issue a £100 fixed penalty notice. Noise abatement notices allow for similar interventions.

Parenting contracts and orders: Contracts can set out the roles of both the parent and youth offending teams in order to improve the anti-social behaviour of a young person. If contracts are not adhered to, then orders can be sought in court; failure to adhere to orders is a criminal offence.

Suspended possession orders: A court order making eviction possible for anti-social behaviour.

There has been a flurry of activity in response to this perceived rise in anti-social behaviour and at the time this conditionality proposal was put forward, many new policies had already been implemented or have been subsequently introduced.

Besides the political imperative, another reason for seeking to tackle anti-social behaviour is that it appears to have a disproportionately high effect on more deprived communities. The British Crime Survey (2000) reported that council tenants were more likely to perceive that they lived in areas of high disorder especially if they lived in low-income and/or multi-ethnic areas. They were also more likely to perceive that the disorder has a negative impact on their quality of life. Research by Hunter *et al.* (2000) analysed the case files of tenants who were the subject of complaints and found over ninety per cent were in receipt of benefits. According to the Chartered Institute of Housing, although social renters are no more likely to be victims of anti-social behaviour than owner-occupiers and, if anything, the likelihood of being a victim increases with income, where quality of life is already degraded by a lack of income, other discomforts are likely to take on greater significance. If this policy reduced anti-social behaviour in deprived areas it could be justified on the grounds of enhancing equality of opportunity.

The proposal can also be said to be based on the social democratic value of civility. The rationale that was given for the proposal was that the prospect of a sanction would prevent people from behaving anti-socially, partly by sending a strong signal about the unacceptability of anti-social behaviour, but would also act as a penalty on those who were not deterred. The Department for Work and Pensions (DWP 2003a:1) put it this way: 'we sympathise with those who question whether the state should support the housing costs of people whose behaviour brings misery to the lives of individuals and communities'. It was argued by the Home Office that this measure would be capable of being applied quickly and decisively and be practical and usable, that it would be fair and be seen to be fair, and would reduce social exclusion.

A wide range of organisations, however, objected to this proposal on grounds of principle. For example, the Child Poverty Action Group said:

> We do not believe it is possible to weigh rights to benefits against responsible behaviour without undermining the basis on which social security operates. The purpose of welfare benefits is to provide a safety net, and should not be used as a tool for punishment. (Child Poverty Action Group 2003)

This highlights a key tension between the use of benefit sanctions and the need to maintain a minimum safety net of income and housing. If people already living at that minimum are sanctioned, what are they to do then? The rationale test can be said to have been passed on the grounds of increasing equality of opportunity and civility but this reservation is significant although not necessarily decisive.

Test two: evidence

This proposal was dropped as a result of significant opposition from a wide range of bodies, not necessarily because the Government ceased to think it was a good idea. This makes it worth exploring the evidence to see if the policy could reasonably be expected to reduce anti-social behaviour and enhance civility.

The primary argument that the proposal would fail to reduce anti-social behaviour is that the policy would not deal with the root causes of this type of behaviour. For example, research by the Social Exclusion Unit (2000) and others has identified that perpetrators of anti-social behaviour often face a complex range of problems including poverty, unemployment and drug dependency and this proposal would do nothing to address these things. A Home Office review of ASBOs in 2002 found that in over sixty per cent of cases there were mitigating factors such as mental ill health, addiction, learning difficulties and school exclusion.

This objection draws attention to the fact that this particular conditionality proposal is different from the work-related conditions on the out-of-work benefits considered above where the condition imposed has a direct relationship to the benefit it impacts. This qualitative difference was raised by a number of organisations in the consultation on the proposal. It was argued that the link between the offence and the punishment would be too remote because there is no direct link between behaviour and housing. For example, the Local Government Association said:

> Behaviour is not material to the primary conditions of entitlement to housing benefit in the same way that failure to comply with a job-seeking direction may affect entitlement to unemployment benefit. (Local Government Association 2003)

It seems reasonable to argue that there needs to be a clear link between the sanction and the type of behaviour it is seeking to address, for example sanctions on failing to seek work where the aim of the benefit is to provide security while a person looks for work, as in the case of JobSeeker's Allowance. Following this reasoning, conditionality for altering anti-social behaviour ought to be linked to a provision that tackles the underlying causes of that behaviour. There is certainly an argument that financial incentives and sanctions do not make sense in relation to non-economic (and often non-rational) behaviour such as anti-social behaviour. This argument on its own may not be decisive but it raises significant doubts about the potential of Housing Benefit sanctions to impact anti-social behaviour and suggests there are limits to the applicability of welfare conditionality.

Whilst the evidence from social psychology is not conclusive and can only be suggestive about the likely impact of Housing Benefit sanctions, a survey of the evidence does point to the likelihood that placing conditions on the receipt of benefit will impact behaviour (Crossfield 2004). However, it also suggests that rewards are likely to have a more positive impact than sanctions, as sanctioning could lead to resistance against the authority instigating the sanction, but that even rewards will not always be effective. In order to increase the likelihood of effectiveness, the evidence suggests that the way conditions are imposed needs to be perceived to be just.

The Home Office did acknowledge that in order to be effective the regime must be fair and be seen to be fair. Fairness, or the perception of justice, has a number of components. Social psychology reveals that people do not only consider the outcomes of justice (distributive justice), but also the process of justice (procedural justice) and the quality of interpersonal treatment they receive from an authority figure during the enactment of processes (interactional justice) in assessing the justice of their experience. For example, the procedural fairness of individual encounters with representatives of public services have been found to affect the overall evaluation of how well that agency is serving the public (Sunshine and Tyler 2003). Non-compliance is a likely response to perceived injustice. This means there must be a highly effective administration system in place so that people do not experience unfair sanctioning or a sense of injustice which may undermine the effectiveness of the sanctioning regime.

Despite the Home Office's assertion that this policy would be practical and usable, a number of issues were raised about possible difficulties which may be encountered in implementing this policy that highlight risks around its perceived justice. The administrative option for implementing the policy would have given a high level of discretion to an unaccountable local authority officer without independent scrutiny, which raises concerns over a possible lack of consistency in the application of the sanction, although this objection may be overcome through the inclusion of independent oversight.

Concerns were also raised that the administration of Housing Benefit is notoriously poor and such a policy would further complicate the system by generating additional bureaucracy, expense and mistakes. Difficulties over the definition of anti-social behaviour also raise risks around a lack of fairness and disproportionate responses. Under the definition used by the Home Office, there is a possibility of the same sanction being applied in cases of continual shouting and those of actual violence.

Social psychology also tells us that behaviour is not just motivated by reward and punishment but also by the degree to which an individual believes an action will lead to a particular change, that is, they have 'self-efficacy'. Research has often shown that ensuring people are able to participate in decisions that affect their lives can result in greater levels of self-efficacy and a belief that they can change things through their own actions. Participation can give people the ability to change things in their communities (Campbell and Jovchelovitch 2000). Raising people's sense of self-efficacy through giving them a sense of participation and control would appear to be a good strategy for affecting behavioural change in relation to anti-social behaviour.

Consideration must also be made of possible unintended consequences. The introduction of the single room rent restriction on Housing Benefit for those aged under twenty five is an example of where the behaviour change that occurred was not the one intended. The restriction was intended to encourage claimants to negotiate a lower rent with their landlord or remain in the family home until they were able to pay housing costs from earned income. But faced with a shortfall of rent to make up, instead claimants fell into rent arrears and/or debt as they borrowed to pay their rent (Phelps and Wheatley 2002).

Even if the Housing Benefit proposal was effective on its own terms, policy makers must also consider its interaction with other policies and any unintended consequences. For example, the Government wants to promote a healthy private rented sector but Shelter (2003) has argued that this conditionality policy would work directly against this objective by deterring private landlords from taking Housing Benefit tenants and acting as an impediment to the market working well.

Whilst this condition might be effective in changing behaviour, it would not be able to tackle the underlying causes of anti-social behaviour and so is unlikely to be successful in the longer term. It is not possible to conclude that the evidence test is passed.

Test three: unfair side effects

This policy could only be applied to people who are in receipt of Housing Benefit, probably the most class-defined benefit. Housing Benefit is disproportionately claimed by people from poor and minority ethnic backgrounds and any further condition on claiming this benefit that other people not claiming it did not have to fulfil could be said to be discriminatory and give rise to the inequitable enforcement of social duties. Whilst anti-social behaviour does appear to be concentrated in deprived areas, there is significant evidence of anti-social behaviour in non-deprived areas and this proposal offers no way of dealing with perpetrators who are not in receipt of Housing Benefit. The Chartered Institute of Housing has suggested that the proposals around extending the conditions on child benefit were quickly dismissed largely because they affected a much wider and more powerful group of people.

However, this inequity need not be a decisive objection according to Stuart White's framework if it leads to sufficient benefit to the disadvantaged and there is no other, politically feasible way of achieving this benefit that does not produce this or a similar inequity. The policy could reduce anti-social behaviour in deprived neighbourhoods and so raise the average quality of life of the most disadvantaged. But this would be achieved at quite considerable cost to those families that are sanctioned. For example, Shelter (2003) predicted that it would lead to homelessness (and these people would be deemed 'intentionally homeless' and therefore not priority for rehousing). The policy may also punish those people who cannot control their behaviour, such as those with mental health issues, or those who are not able to control visitors or family members. It would also impact on innocent third parties. For example, children may be put at risk of eviction as a result of rent arrears due to Housing Benefit sanctions, when the perpetrator of the anti-social behaviour is an adult relation. Frank Field MP – who originally proposed this policy – envisaged that the families in question would be split up, with children going to live with foster parents and adults being consigned to special residential units that are purposively remote from the rest of society. This seems a high price to make these people pay.

Further, in the absence of evidence on outcomes for individuals who are sanctioned and 'rescue strategies' for those sanctioned, other approaches should be considered that could lead to improvement in average prospects and have a smaller risk of creating losers. It is beyond the remit of this report to examine these alternatives in detail (see Edwards forthcoming 2005 for a fuller discussion) as there is a range of options covering the full spectrum from prevention, to intensive support, to the use of the criminal justice system; but it is important to outline briefly some two prominent examples.

The Dundee Families Project and the Shelter Inclusion Project both aim to tackle the root causes of anti-social behaviour and have had some success. The Shelter project works with people in Rochdale with alleged anti-social behaviour. It has identified a range of support needs amongst these families including emotional support, parenting advice, assistance in running a home, support liaising with their landlord and dealing with neighbours and unwelcome visitors (Jones *et al.* 2004). During its first year of operation the project identified the following outcomes:

- successful engagement with the project by people with alleged anti-social behaviour;

- assisting the majority to maintain tenancies;

- a reduction in alleged anti-social behaviour;

- a high level of user satisfaction;

- the support of other agencies.

Deacon (2004) describes the Dundee Families Project, which aims to provide accommodation for families threatened with eviction because of their anti-social behaviour, as follows:

> Whilst participating in the project the families are subject to intensive interventions designed to change their behaviour ... Amongst these ... are regular visits – initially at 'breakfast time, tea time and bed time' – to ensure that the family is maintaining an acceptable lifestyle, and counselling and treatment to deal with issues of mental health, addictions, parenting skills and anger management.

The project takes a multi-disciplinary approach to improving families' situations and social functioning. Deacon reports that the project 'appears to work', citing an evaluation by a team at Glasgow University which concluded that it failed to achieve its objectives in less than one fifth of the cases referred to it. This approach to anti-social behaviour does, of course, also involve conditionality as there are many conditions families must adhere to in order to get on to and remain in the project. These approaches appear to hold out the prospect of reducing anti-social behaviour, and so improve the average quality of life for the disadvantaged, at less risk of harm to those families most likely to be engaged in anti-social behaviour. Of course, they bring the further benefit of the potential to improve the prospects of these families by providing them with the kind of structured and intensive support they need to overcome established patterns of behaviour. The problem with the Housing Benefit proposal lies in the specific form of conditionality proposed – attaching the conditions to benefit receipt, not in the basic principle of conditionality itself.

Similar projects to the Inclusion and Dundee projects are now being set up in other areas but they may prove challenging to replicate very widely because of the difficulties of putting a funding package together. This is despite the fact that those running the Dundee project estimate that – at worst – it costs no more than conventional methods of dealing with anti-social behaviour. Other support measures which are more widespread include tenancy sustainment work and warden support. A recent ippr expert seminar concluded that there is relatively good evidence and understanding of what works in tackling serious problems of nuisance neighbours in the short term, although there is some way to go in encouraging widespread and effective implementation of the tools available (Edwards 2004).

The likelihood of significant harm, weak rescue strategies and better alternatives mean that the unfair side effects test is failed.

5 Evidence of impact on other benefit recipients

The available evidence on the impact of existing conditions on the three groups under consideration here is limited, so it is worth looking at the evidence of the impact of conditions on other benefit claimant groups to assess the possible impacts of any extension of conditions. Evidence is drawn from the evaluations of sanctioning regimes in the New Deal for Young People (NDYP), the New Deal for the Long-Term Unemployed (NDLTU), the community sanctions and benefit withdrawal pilot, the Sure Start Maternity Grant (SSMG) and JSA. The main characteristics of these regimes are summarised in Table 2.4.

Table 2.4 Examples of current or piloted sanctioning regimes

NDYP

Eligible group:	Eighteen to twenty four year-olds after six months' unemployment.
Conditions:	Personal adviser meeting. Four-month 'Gateway' period of intensive support. 'Back to work option' after ten months' unemployment.
Sanctions:	JSA withdrawn or withheld for failure to participate.

NDLTU

Eligible group:	Long-term unemployed aged over twenty five.
Conditions:	Thirteen-week intensive activity period on completion of standard NDLTU Gateway period.
Sanctions:	Benefit sanctions for failure to participate or notify an inability to attend.

JSA 26-week sanctioning regime pilot

Eligible group:	JSA claimants in pilot areas who breach the terms of the New Deal 18-24 or New Deal 25+.
Conditions:	Must: - be willing/ able to take up work - actively seek work - not leave work voluntarily - not unreasonably refuse to take up job interview/offer - not unreasonably refuse to attend prescribed employment programme/ training scheme.
Sanctions:	JSA sanctions for up to twenty six weeks for two breaches of rules, and where received two previous two or four-week sanctions. And thirteen weeks of sanctions on range of benefits for claimants found guilty of benefit fraud on two occasions within three years of having sanctions imposed.

Test one: rationale

The different programmes had a variety of rationale but all aimed to strengthen the responsibilities of benefits claimants – and in some cases their rights. For example, the policy objective of the community sanctions and benefit withdrawal pilot was to link the receipt of benefit more closely to the fulfilment of responsibilities to society and to encourage greater compliance with community sentences (Knight *et al.* 2003), whilst the SSMG aims to improve equality of opportunity of children born into low-income families. The focus here is the evidence of the impact of the policies on behaviour and any possible mixed impacts.

Test two: evidence

The evidence of changed behaviour shows a mixed picture. The evaluation of the community sentencing and benefits withdrawal policy led to only a 1.8 per cent increase in compliance with community punishments among those on relevant benefits (Knight *et al.* 2003). This implies for every fifty sentences given, one fewer resulted in breach initiation as a result of the policy. Offenders reported that they did not see the policy as a major influence on their behaviour. Researchers concluded that the impact of the policy was constrained by limited consciousness of it and attitudes to compliance amongst offenders. The policy had less potential to influence non-compliance where there were difficult personal issues, substance abuse, a rejection of probation or little personal motivation to comply. Some offenders reported additional or renewed offending which they linked directly with the policy.

In the JSA basic skills pilots attendance rates were substantially higher in areas piloting sanctions and incentives compared with areas that were not. Sanctions and incentives did seem to generate a change in behaviour and increase attendance in basic skills training but there was less evidence of improved outcomes as a result of that change in behaviour. Respondents who had started the training were no more likely to have found work since the Jobcentre screening than those who had not attended. However, there did appear to have been an impact on people's confidence in their future job prospects. Of those who had started a course and found a job, over a third said the course had helped them get the job, although the majority said it had not helped.

A study of disallowed and sanctioned JSA claimants found that sanctioning resulted in a loss of trust in Jobcentre staff and people saying they would never sign on again, or would be more guarded or lie to staff in future (Vincent 1998). These people said they did not fully understand the rules and blamed staff for the inconsistencies they thought they had heard. It also found that whilst some people had become more cautious in the jobs they would consider, others had widened their efforts to find work.

A study of the twenty six-week sanctioning regime found that sanctions reinforced existing reasons to comply for some, but had less potential to influence non-compliance that related to chaotic or unmanaged personal lives, problematic substance use, rejection of authority and the absence of personal motivation (Dhillon 2000). It found that sanctioning resulted in only a small number of claimants agreeing to widen their job search activities. Again, it found that others became more cautious about the type of job they would accept and some felt their personal circumstances had made their disallowance unavoidable and they could not behave differently in future. By November 2002, 2.2 per cent of the eligible caseload had been sanctioned or disallowed.

The evidence from the NDYP sanctioning regime was more positive; it suggested that sanctions did bring about a greater level of compliance than might otherwise have occurred and an increase in job seeking activity. In a study by O'Connor and others (2001), interviewees reported that the threat of benefit sanctions was a motivating factor to comply with the requirements of the programme. The threat of reduced income, however temporary, acted as a disincentive for many to refuse take-up of an option or to depart from an option prematurely; although the benefits of escaping from an unsatisfactory option did at times far outweigh the potential impact of any financial penalty.

These evaluations of the sanctioning regimes reveal some of the reasons why they failed to bring about the desired behavioural change. Three broad classes of reasons for non-compliance emerge:

- Deliberate non-compliance as a result of specific dissatisfaction with the actions required usually resulting from a lack of choice in selecting activities or broader rejection of regime.

- Unwitting non-compliance as a result of limited or mistaken knowledge about the rules. In particular people resented being mandated onto a programme they did not feel would enhance their job prospects.

- A result of a claimant's personal circumstances that militate against or prevent compliance, such as a chaotic lifestyle.

Nearly all people interviewed by O'Connor and others (2001) thought there should be rules backed up by penalties in the benefits system but that the rules should be flexible to take account of particular circumstances, and applied with compassion. In reality respondents felt there were inconsistencies in their treatment and the reasons for their behaviour were not always taken into account. The researchers found that the threat of a reduction in benefit was commonly accepted among the young people and perceived to be part of life on unemployment benefit. However, where a young person had young dependants, it was felt that the imposition of benefit sanctions was unjustified. Experience of sanctions also generated a lot of anger and frustration where participants felt they had been unfairly treated. Psychological distress was reported as people felt demotivated in their job search or lacking in confidence after incurring sanctions. It was felt that people should not be forced to compromise their aspirations by taking 'any job' when they could be doing something better. There were concerns that the approach could result in young people embarking on option placements that were not appropriate for them or had little interest in pursuing. In the long run this was believed to be counterproductive.

It is clear that the process and the perceived justice of that process was crucial in bringing about compliance. Personal advisers themselves tended to agree with the principle of matching rights with responsibilities but were critical about the processes involved. They reported that sanctioning processes were administratively complex and hard to implement. There was variation between personal advisers in the nature of decisions referred for adjudication in cases of non-compliance resulting in potential variation in the application of the rules. Personal advisers generally thought sanctions were too blunt an instrument with which to deal with certain categories of claimant such as those with chaotic lifestyles. There was anxiety that the programme might intensify social exclusion.

The evidence of the success of extended conditionality in bringing about changes in behaviour capable of delivering improved outcomes is mixed. It is clear that the perceived justice of the implementation of the regime is critical to its success and that the personal adviser/client relationship is pivotal and steps must be taken to protect its integrity. The evidence test shows that there are reasonable grounds to suppose that extended conditions can change behaviour but if these changes are to deliver improved outcomes then careful attention must be paid to implementation and communication.

Test three: unfair side effects

Did these programmes lead to inequity in the enforcement of social duties? All welfare to work programmes imply the enforcement of the social duty to enter paid employment, which is clearly not applied equally across the social spectrum. However, this is acceptable provided clear benefits are delivered to disadvantaged groups by the policy and the policy does not lead to unacceptable further inequity within the disadvantaged group. Bonjour and others (2001) found that disadvantaged groups were no more likely to experience sanctions or benefit penalties in the NDYP than other entrants, except in the case of those with basic skills problems. Staff implementing the twenty six-week JSA regime reported concerns about the fairness of the policy imposing an additional penalty on benefit recipients that others had not experienced. Staff implementing the community sanctions regime had concerns it would increase marginalisation for some types of offender such as those with fewest personal resources to cope with the sanction.

The other main impact of the programmes was financial. The financial impact of the NDYP and NDLTU sanctions was variable, primarily depending on the extent to which the sanctioned persons had access to alternative forms of financial support (O'Connor *et al.* 2000; Molloy and Ritchie 2000). Sanctions had most impact on individuals who were themselves parents, on those who were living alone without access to informal sources of support, or those who were dealing with difficult personal issues, such as debt, homelessness or drug dependency. In these cases there were recurrent accounts of not having enough money to buy food or electricity and increased debt could also occur because of benefit sanction. Sanctioned JSA claimants with children reported strong emotions with feelings of anger and outrage, depression and fear being common (Vincent 1998). Where young people lived in rented accommodation, rent arrears were a typical side effect. Sanctioned participants of the twenty six-week JSA regime experienced debt, general hardship and arrears. The impact varied widely, with those with literacy problems, problems with drugs and/or alcohol, a criminal record or who were homeless being less likely to report having obtained alternative benefits or payments (Bonjour *et al.* 2000).

In most cases sanctioned clients can apply for hardship payments during the sanctioned period which can help to ease the experience. Nonetheless, these are all worrying consequences and the unfair side effects test cannot be said to have been passed although the availability of hardship grants is a possible 'rescue strategy' to help mitigate these effects.

The mixed evidence on the success of these programmes in achieving their

Australia's review of sanctioning policies

In 2001 a review was undertaken into Australia's sanctioning regime because of 'concerns that the system for achieving compliance with obligations imposed on people ... was not operating equitably and effectively in regard to all recipients'. There had been an overall increase in the incidence of breaching of conditions of three hundred per cent in the three years to August 2001.

The review found that on many occasions the operation of the regime was 'arbitrary, unfair or excessively harsh' and on many occasions it diminished people's capacity and opportunity to continue seeking work and become less dependent on social security.

The issues identified by the review highlight some of the potential risks in implementing a sanctioning regime. These included:

- poor communication with jobseekers and between agencies;
- inappropriate selection of job search activities;
- sanctioning occurring without sufficient investigation and consideration of individual circumstances;
- severe penalties, causing unnecessary and unjustifiable hardship;
- undue rigidity in design and implementation;
- insufficient provision of time and appropriate training for staff;
- not looking at the cause of failure of compliance.

Source: Pearce, Disney and Ridout 2002

aims suggests their outcomes are far from overwhelming and in some cases the regime actually militated against people moving into employment or coming into compliance by making them more wary and less inclined to engage positively with Jobcentre staff and experience a strong sense of injustice.

6 Public opinion

Strengthening public support for the benefits system is a key motivation for the Government to introduce extended conditions on benefits, which makes it important to consider briefly the evidence on the thrust of public opinion on these issues.

Overall, a high level of support can be detected for the welfare state. During the 1990s people were more likely to say they would prefer an increase in taxes to fund more spending on health, education and social benefits than to keep taxes and spending the same or reduce them (Williams *et al.* 1999). However, there appears to be much less support for welfare spending on lone parents and unemployed people than for other groups, even amongst those who support more spending on the poor (British Attitudes Survey 2000). People's level of knowledge and understanding of the benefit system is generally poor and the British Attitudes Survey shows that people grossly overestimate welfare spending on unemployed people and lone parents. There is also a strong sense of the 'deserving' and 'undeserving' benefit recipients. These kinds of reservations and distinctions appear to represent a hardening of attitudes towards benefits. This may be partly driven by the trend for people to be less sympathetic to welfare spending when the economy is stronger.

A qualitative study undertaken by Peter Dwyer found that a slim majority of people (fifty one per cent) were in favour of making unemployment benefit more conditional and linking unemployed people's right to benefit to additional work or training conditions (Dwyer 2000). However, it should be noted that this study was undertaken in 1997 and so it cannot give any indication of the impact of New Labour's approach to welfare on public opinion. Support for benefit conditions was based on a set of three beliefs:

- additional work or training conditions would give people more skills and help them re-enter the labour market;

- unemployed people should be charged with the responsibility to make some form of contribution to society in return for their right to benefit;

- such measures could help to counter the body of people who did not try to find work.

But support for extended conditionality was contingent on the scheme being well implemented and administered in that it took account of people's wider social circumstances. The forty three per cent of people who strongly opposed extended conditions in this study based their views on three key beliefs:

- extended conditions were unnecessary;

- the state would be better occupied in promoting an environment in which there were sufficient numbers of suitable jobs available;

- sceptism about the motives for mandating work, suspecting it was a way of getting 'work done on the cheap'.

Instead, these people preferred policies that encouraged people into work by assisting them and felt compulsion would be counterproductive. One respondent said: 'If they are trying to create a new work ethic where people want to work, then you are not going to do that by forcing people into it' (Dwyer 2000:152).

There is no consensus that lone parents should be in employment and there is only limited support for policies that would require or compel them to enter paid work. As Millar says: 'public attitudes towards mothers' employment in the UK are contingent upon circumstances, and there is no agreement that paid work is always the best option' (Millar 2003:119). Half the people in one study believed lone parents should be able to choose for themselves whether to go out to work (Hills and Leikes quoted in Millar 2003).

The age of children appears to underpin views on whether lone parents should be required to work. One survey found that six in ten adults believed a mother with a pre-school child should not work outside the home at all, in fact, twenty four per cent believed she has a duty to stay at home (Hills and Leikes quoted in Millar 2003). Most people (eighty one per cent) tended to think that lone parents of school age children should work, however, only eleven per cent believed this employment should be full-time. In Dwyer's study nearly half the respondents thought that lone mothers with school-age children have a duty to go out to work. In February 2004, only one-fifth of lone parents claiming Income Support had a youngest child of secondary school age, so imposing work requirements on this group would affect a relatively small proportion of all lone parents and not change the status quo dramatically.

In Dwyer's study there was strong support for encouraging claimants of Incapacity Benefit back to work – where that was feasible. Generally, though, this support did not extend to making job search activity a condition of claiming Incapacity Benefit claimants and the preference was for an approach that would encourage and help people to work, rather than compel them to do so. People also distinguished between disabled people who were willing but unable to work and those who were simply unwilling – the former were seen as more deserving than others.

On housing issues the most prevalent view shared by the majority of participants in Dwyer's study was that the right to a house should be contingent on tenants behaving themselves, and those with a persistent disregard for their neighbours should be evicted. However, support for a more conditional regime was dependent on the manner in which policy was implemented and that people received warning before action was taken. Several groups, however, resented the assumption that behaviour is always exclusively the outcome of an individual making some kind of socially isolated rational decision. They argued that individual behaviour is often grounded in a particular social, cultural or environmental context and that educating people about the potential harm was a better way to proceed. From this limited evidence (gathered before anti-social behaviour issues really came into the spotlight) there appear to be mixed views of rights and responsibilities in housing, but support for conditionality is clearly predicated on a number of conditions being met and questions were not asked explicitly about benefit sanctions for anti-social behaviour.

On the basis of this evidence it is not possible to identify a clear demand from the public that extended conditions should be imposed on lone parents, disabled people or anti-social tenants although there is clear support for a broad framework of rights and responsibilities and conditions being placed on those who are in a position to fulfil them. There is an urgent need for this gap in the evidence to be filled.

Section 3

Policy implications

Kate Stanley

Lone parents

On the basis of the analysis presented here it would be possible to recommend the extension of work-related requirements on lone parents' receipt of out-of-work benefits so that they are required actively to seek and take up a job, if the job met certain pre-agreed flexibility requirements and appropriate childcare was available.

Lone parents with disabled children or children with special needs would need to be exempted. Lone parents who were not work-ready or wanted to enhance their progression opportunities would need to be able to choose full-time education or training (with the Government offering a financial support package) instead of work-search activity.

However, in order to be effective and just this policy proposal would require a number of conditions to be met:

- Further improvement in the childcare infrastructure so that affordable, accessible, high quality childcare was widely available (if not the policy would mean only limited numbers of lone parents were able to take up work and the policy would be more complex to administer).

- Substantial in-work financial support so that policy did not contribute to a rise in the numbers of working households living in poverty and to help make childcare affordable.

- Generous out-of-work support to lone parents to ensure that children of lone parents who were not in work, as a result of exemptions, for example, were not disadvantaged by living in poverty.

- Continuing stability and relative security in the labour market in which suitable jobs are available.

- Additional capacity in Jobcentre Plus to delivery WFIs and to commission the delivery of NDLP and other welfare to work programmes offering individual advice, support and work-search guidance to a greater number of lone parents.

- Flexibility in the application of rules. Some of the mandated clients will be 'harder to help' and certain rules could cause harm if applied without fully taking into account a person's circumstances. Providers need the decision-making authority to apply the rules appropriately and the skills and training to ensure the proper exercise of that authority.

■ Participants given a say in the kind of service they receive, making the balance between rights and responsibilities clearer and more meaningful.

It would be necessary that such a policy only applied to lone parents with children aged eleven or over. This is because it would be prudent to pilot the policy first and this would be the most appropriate group to pilot the policy with because:

■ primary school hours are shorter and it would be challenging to find work to fit around these hours without flexible and readily available childcare and/or extended schools;

■ public opinion seems to be more supportive of conditionality for parents with children aged eleven or over;

■ the infrastructure of Jobcentre Plus and its provider networks might struggle to meet the demands of a larger group of mandated clients and the service might suffer as a result.

There are three key benefits to this policy, starting with the most important for social democrats.

Improved child outcomes
The potential gain is significant in terms of reducing the numbers of workless households and thereby reducing child poverty. Over half a million children stand to move out of workless households and there is evidence that outcomes for children are better where adults in the household are in work. Paid work can also have positive impacts for the lone parents in terms of self-esteem, confidence and well-being, which can bring benefits for their children.

Benefits to the economy
Continued stable economic growth is premised on further increases in the participation of women in the paid labour market. Greater efforts to improve pay and conditions and progression routes in the labour market might further increase female employment rates and generate greater dynamism in the labour market. In most of the rest of western Europe there is greater conditionality and higher rates of lone parent employment. This suggests the policy might work.

Boosting public support for welfare
The policy would be in step with public opinion and European trends. It could enhance public support for the welfare system and help de-stigmatise lone parents by emphasising responsibilities and economic reciprocity.

However, there are three powerful arguments against the policy which must also be considered.

Given limited resources and capacity in Jobcentre Plus, there is a need to prioritise. Delivering extended work-related conditionality policies on lone parents of children aged eleven and over would be a distraction from delivering improved employment support to disabled people, a much larger and more diverse group.

The policy has been assessed here against social democratic criteria but it is also worth noting that the savings from lone parent conditionality are unlikely to be very substantial given the need to couple conditionality with enhanced childcare and in-work support and so on. The work-related requirements would also be potentially complex to administer and monitor. They would be resource-intensive given the need for certain provisions such as ensuring appropriate childcare is available in order to mitigate risks to children's welfare. Such caveats may also further reduce the number of people who could move into work despite the programme.

Unnecessary risks

Lone parent employment rates have increased more than rates for all other groups with a labour market disadvantage, without extended conditionality. The NDLP appears to be working. Its success is significantly attributable to the positive relationships that personal advisers have been able to build with their clients, which rest on the willingness of clients to volunteer, and personal advisers being seen as there to help rather than there to enforce rules. Conditionality would put this success at risk. Current strategies do appear to have been effective in increasing the employment rate of lone parents and extended conditionality would put these successes at risk.

Entrenching labour market inequalities

Employment does not ensure social inclusion, this depends on the quality of work offered. The jobs that lone parents would be most likely to move into would tend to be low-paying and offer poor progression opportunities. This could further entrench inequalities in the labour market and deliver weak gains in terms of reducing child poverty and enhancing the well-being of parents. There is a risk that those with more barriers to work are sanctioned, bringing stigma and making them harder to employ.

Conditionality policies would also face difficulties in accommodating the strong care ethos which is apparent amongst lone parents who may be choosing not to work as a result of their understanding of what is best for their children.

On balance it is reasonable to propose the piloting of the extension of conditionality to lone parents. However, implementing the policy in a way that minimised risk and supported lone parents in reasonably secure jobs with some opportunities for progression would require a very significant resources and bring limited savings in Income Support expenditure. This would mean that there were fewer resources available to focus on the biggest challenge where least progress has been made to date – the employment of disabled people.

Disabled people

Work-related conditions on IB should not be extended for three key reasons.

Inadequate policy foundations
The policy framework of the incapacity benefits regime is unable to respond adequately to the need to support more disabled people into work and provide support to those for whom work is not an option, thereby enhancing equality of opportunity.

There is a need to reform incapacity benefits, and in particular IB, to resolve the central paradox at the heart of any attempt to link IB and work conditions. Current disability benefit policy falsely equates disability with incapacity. In order to be eligible to claim IB a person must demonstrate their incapacity to work; so requiring that they seek work would be absurd. The simultaneous policy drive both to protect people from the consequences of a proscribed access to employment and to move them off benefit dependency and into employment cannot be adequately addressed within the current framework. If work conditions were applied to IB, it would remove the rationale for having IB at all, which is to identify the population for whom participating in paid work is not a reasonable requirement.

Identifying capacity for work
It is extremely difficult to make the distinction between those for whom work is not an option at a given point, and those for whom some form of work is possible. The medicalised assessment of eligibility for IB is inadequate for making this more nuanced determination. This difficulty would make extended work-related conditions difficult and high risk to implement.

A sophisticated assessment of capacity for work requires assessment of a person's impairment, their wider personal circumstances, an understanding of the jobs available and the capacities they require. The methods to deliver such an assessment are under-developed and rehabilitation professionals and occupational therapists are not available to be able to deliver it.

Lack of evidence of what works for whom
The evidence base on what works for whom in supporting disabled people into work is very limited. This is partly because until very recently little had

been done to support disabled people into work at all and few resources have been put into developing active labour market programmes for disabled people. The Pathways to Work pilots themselves only began in 2003. The early findings from these pilots are promising and evidence-based policy making requires that the evaluations of these pilots are understood before any significant changes to welfare to work policy are made.

Instead of extending work conditions on IB, there is a need for a four-pronged approach to enhancing equality of opportunity for disabled people through the steps outlined below:

Reform incapacity benefits
Incapacity benefits – and IB, in particular – should be reformed in order to resolve their inability to respond to the need to support more disabled people into work and provide support to those for whom work is not an option that ensures they do not live in poverty.

Tackle supply side barriers
The low employment rate of disabled people is not simply a matter of motivation or even impairment barriers, but the result of the interaction of a person's impairment with the wider environment. This means environmental barriers such as inaccessible transport and employer discrimination must also be tackled. The forthcoming Disability Bill, full implementation of the Disability Discrimination Act and the creation of the Commission for Equality and Human Rights will all have a role to play in this.

Provide individually tailored help for disabled people to enter work and stay in work
Individualised job search advice and guidance appears to be the most effective way of supporting disabled people to find work. Increasing in-work support would help ensure work pays and sharpen the incentives for those who can to move into work. The right support would also help ensure disabled people are able to sustain employment. This may include the rollout of Pathways to Work if the evaluation evidence supports this.

Widen the concept of participation
The concepts of participation and citizenship need to be widened so that worth is not simply defined by labour market participation but that formal and informal social and economic activity are all components of active citizenship. The current rhetoric around paid work and rights and responsibilities could undermine the legitimacy of benefits paid without economic reciprocity such as IB and diminish the self-worth of those for whom paid work is not possible. This is a more positive and inclusive formulation of rights and responsibilities than the current exclusive orientation around paid work.

Anti-social tenants

Behaviour-based conditions should not be attached to Housing Benefit for four key reasons:

Root causes
Housing Benefit sanctions would not address the root causes of anti-social behaviour. These root causes include poverty, unemployment and drug dependency.

Perceptions of justice
It would be extremely difficult to implement the policy in a way that was just and seen to be just. For example, it could only be applied to people in receipt of Housing Benefit and offers no way of dealing with people who behave anti-socially and are not receiving Housing Benefit. It would also be complex to administer it in a way that was seen to be fair, partly because of the existing complexities in the Housing Benefit administration system, and the wide definition of anti-social behaviour.

Risk of harm
The policy would run a high risk of causing harm, including to innocent third parties, and exacerbating social exclusion. For example, the policy could lead to homelessness for children or to those who are not able to control the behaviour of others in their household.

Better alternatives
There are viable alternatives that would achieve the same objective without the attendant risks. A range of tools is available and the Government should support more holistic interventions.

This does not mean that it is inappropriate to use conditionality policies in relation to anti-social behaviour, indeed conditionality is a crucial policy tool. For example, in programmes that take a supportive and holistic approach to anti-social behaviour, the inclusion of a household in the programme is conditional on their abiding by its terms. It simply means that sanctioning Housing Benefit as a result of anti-social behaviour is inappropriate.

Conclusion: Conditionality as a policy tool

Applying a social democratic framework to three specific policy proposals demonstrates the limitations of benefit conditionality and shows that it is not an appropriate tool for achieving certain outcomes. Extended conditionality can often be justified using social democratic rationale and there are grounds for thinking extended benefit conditions can bring about behavioural change. However, there is a more positive conceptualisation of rights and responsibilities than 'pure' extended conditionality implies, one in which people are supported to fulfil their responsibilities and society acknowledges its own responsibilities to disadvantaged people.

References

Adams, G. and Rohacek, M. (2002) *Child Care and Welfare Reform* Policy Brief 14, Urban Institute

Anderson, E. (1999) 'What is the Point of Equality?' in *Ethics* 109: 287–337

Andersson, F., Lane, J. and McEntarfer, E. (2004) *Successful Transitions out of Low-wage Work for Temporary Assistance for Needy Families Recipients* Urban Institute

Bandura, A. (1995) 'Exercise of Personal and Collective Efficacy in Changing Societies' in Bandura, A. (ed) *Self-efficacy in Changing Societies* Cambridge University Press

Berthoud, R. (2003) *Multiple Disadvantage in Employment* Joseph Rowntree Foundation

Beveridge, W. (1942) *Social Insurance and Allied Services* HMSO

Blank, R. (2002) *US Welfare Reform: What's Relevant for Europe?* CESifo Working Paper 753, Centre for Economic Studies and Institute for Economic Research

Blank, R. and Haskins, R. (eds) (2001) *The New World of Welfare* Brookings Institution

Bloom, D., Farrell, M., Fink, B. and Adams-Ciardullo, D. (2002) *Welfare Time Limits: State Policies, Implementation, and Effects on Families* MDRC

Bloom, D. and Winstead, D. (2002) 'Sanctions and Welfare Reform' in *Welfare Reform and Beyond* Policy Brief 12, Brookings Institution

Bogdanor, A. (2004) *Not Working: Why Workfare should replace the New Deal* Policy Exchange

Bonjour, D., Dorsett, R., Knight, G., Lissenburgh, S., Mukherjee, A., Payne, J., Range, M., Urwin, P. and White, M. (2001) *New Deal for Young People: National Survey of Participants: Stage 2*, Research Report 67, Employment Service

Bovenberg, A. (2000) 'Reforming Social Insurance in the Netherlands' in *International Tax and Public Finance* 7: 345–368

Brewer, M., Clark, T. and Wakefield, M. (2002) *Five Years of Social Security Reform in the UK* WP02/12 Institute for Fiscal Studies

Brown, G. (2004) 'Chancellor's Speech Budget 2004' Available at www.hmtreasury.gov.uk

Buchel, F., Mertens, A. and Orsini, K. (2003) *Is Mothers' Employment an Effective Means to Fight Family Poverty? Empirical Evidence from Seven European Countries* Luxembourg Income Study Working Paper Series

Burchardt, T. (2000) *Ending Economic Exclusion: Disability, Income and Work* Centre for Analysis of Social Exclusion

Cabinet Office 'Improving the Life Chances of Disabled People' Project briefing given 14th September 2004, Prime Minister's Strategy Unit

Campbell, C. and Jovchelovitch, S. (2000) 'Health, Community and Development: Towards a Social Psychology of Participation' in *Journal of Community and Applied Social Psychology* 10(4): 255–270

Campbell, N., Maniha, J. and Rolston, H. (2002) *Job Retention and Advancement in Welfare Reform* Policy Brief 18, Brookings Institute

Campbell, S. (2002) *A Review of Anti-social Behaviour Orders* Research Study 236, Home Office

Chase-Lansdale, P., Levine Coley, R., Lohman, B. and Pittman, L. (2002) 'Welfare Reform: What About Children?' in *Welfare, Children, and Families* Policy Brief 02–1, Johns Hopkins University

Child Poverty Action Group (2003) *Response to the Home Office White Paper on Anti-Social Behaviour* CPAG

Considine, M. (2001) *Enterprising States: The Public Management of Welfare-to-Work* Cambridge University Press

Crossfield, J. (2004) 'A Psychological Comment on Extending Conditions of Benefits' Background paper prepared for ippr, unpublished

Daly, M. and Burkhauser, R. (2003) *Left Behind: SSI in the Era of Welfare Reform* Working Paper 2003-12, Federal Reserve Bank of San Francisco

Deacon, A. (2000) 'Learning from the US? The influence of American Ideas upon New Labour thinking on Welfare Reform' in *Policy and Politics* 28(1):5–18

Deacon, A. (2002) *Perspectives on Welfare* Open University Press

Deacon, A. (2003a) 'Levelling the Playing Field, Activating the Players. New Labour and the Cycle of Disadvantage' in *Policy and Politics* 31(2):123–138

Deacon, A. (2003b) 'Social Security Policy' in Ellison, N. and Pierson, C. (eds) *Developments in British Social Policy 2* Palgrave Macmillan

Deacon, A. (2004), 'Justifying Conditionality: The Case of Anti-Social Tenants', *Housing Studies* 19(6):911–926

Denham, J. (2004) 'The Fairness Code' in *Prospect* June 2004

Department for Social Security (1998) *Ambitions for our Country: A New Contract for Welfare* DSS

Department for Work and Pensions (2001) *National Benefits Review* DWP

Department for Work and Pensions (2002) *Pathways to Work: helping people into employment* DWP

Department for Work and Pensions (2003) *Quarterly Statistics* DWP

Department for Work and Pensions (2003a) *Housing Benefit Sanctions and Anti-Social Behaviour – A consultation paper* DWP

Department for Work and Pensions (2004a) *Client Group Analysis: Quarterly Bulletin on the Population of Working Aged on Key Benefits* DWP

Department for Work and Pensions (2004b) *Building on New Deal: Local Solutions Meeting Individual Needs, Preliminary Paper* DWP

Department for Work and Pensions (2004c) *Families and Children in Britain: Findings from the 2002 Families and Children Study* DWP

Dhillon, B. (2000), 'Minimising JSA sanctions', *Working Brief* 115, June 2000. Available online at http://www.cesi.org.uk/_newsite2002/publications/wb/w115/html/jsasanctions.htm

Disability Rights Commission (DRC) (2004) Bulletin 31, August 2004 DRC

Dworkin, G. (1971) 'Paternalism' in Wasserstrom, R. (ed.) *Morality and the Law* Wadsworth

Dwyer, P. (2000) *Welfare Rights and Responsibilities* Policy Press

Dwyer, P. (2004) 'Creeping Conditionality in the UK: From Welfare Rights to Conditional Entitlements', *Canadian Journal of Sociology* 29(2)

Edwards, L. (2004) 'Neighbours from Hell?' Report of seminar available at www.ippr.org/research

Ellison, N., and Pierson, C. (2203) 'Introduction: Developments in British Social Policy' in Ellison, N and Pierson, C (eds.) *Developments in British Social Policy 2* Palgrave

Evans, M. (2001) *Welfare to Work and the Organisation of Opportunity: Lessons from Abroad*. CASE report 15, ESRC Research Centre for Analysis of Social Exclusion

Field, F. (2003) *Neighbours from Hell: The Politics of Behaviour* Politico's

Finegold, K. and Wherry, L. (2004) *Race, Ethnicity, and Economic Well-Being Snapshots of America's Families III*. No.19, The Urban Institute

Greenberg, D., Ashworth, K., Cebulla, A. and Walker, R. (2004) 'Do Welfare-to-Work-Programmes Work for Long?' in *Fiscal Studies*. 25(1):27–53

Gregg, P. and Harkness, S. (2003) *Welfare Reform and Lone Parents' Employment in the UK* CMPO Working Paper Series No. 03/072, University of Bristol

Halpern, D. and Bates, C. with Beales, G. and Heathfield, A. (2004) *Personal Responsibility and Changing Behaviour: The State of Knowledge and its Implications for Public Policy* Prime Minister's Strategy Unit

Hamilton, G. (2002) *Moving People from Welfare to Work: Lessons from the National Evaluation of Welfare-to-Work Strategies* MDRC

Haskins, R. and Primus, W. (2001) *Welfare Reform and Poverty* Welfare Reform and Poverty Brief 4, Brookings Institution

HM Treasury (2004) *Budget 2004* Available at www.hmtreasury.gov.uk

Hobhouse, L.T. (1993) [1911] in Meadowcroft, J. (ed.) *Liberalism and Other Writings* Cambridge University Press

Hogelund, J. and Pedersen, J.G. (2002) *Active Labour Market Policies for Disabled People*, Open Labour Market Working Paper 18, Danish National Institute of Social Research

Home Office (2003) *Respect and Responsibility – Taking a Stand Against Anti-Social Behaviour White Paper on Anti-Social Behaviour* The Stationery Office

Howard, M. (2003) An Interactionist Perspective on Barriers and Bridges to work for Disabled People, published at www.ippr.org/research/socialpolicy/disabilityandwork

Howard, M. (2004) *Tax Credits* Child Poverty Action Group

Hunter, C. and Nixon, J. (2002) 'Anti-social Behaviour and Housing' in *Safer Society* spring 2002

Hunter, C., Nixon, J. and Shayer, S. (2000) *Neighbourhood Nuisance, Social Landlords and the Law* JRF and Chartered Institute of Housing

Jones, A., Pleace, N. and Quilgars, D. (2004) *Shelter Inclusion Project: Interim Evaluation Findings* Shelter

King, D. (1999) *In the Name of Liberalism: Illiberal Social Policy in Britain and the United States* Oxford University Press

King, D. and Wickham-Jones, M. (1999) 'From Clinton to Blair: The Democratic (Party) Origins of Welfare to Work' in *The Political Quarterly* 70:62–74

Knight, G. and Lissenburgh, S. (2004) *Evaluation of Lone Parent Work Focused Interviews: Final Findings from Administrative Data Analysis* DWP

Knight, T., Mowlam, A., Woodfield, K., Lewis, J., Purdon, S. and Kitchen, S. with Roberts, C. (2003) *Evaluation of the Community Sentences and Withdrawal of Benefits Pilots* Research Report 98, DWP

Knijn, T. and van Wel, F. (2001) 'Careful or Lenient: Welfare Reform for Lone Mothers in the Netherlands' in *Journal of European Social Policy* 11(3): 235–251(17) Sage Publications

Leira, A. (2002) *Working Parents and the Welfare State – Family Change and Policy Reform in Scandinavia* Cambridge University Press

Leonard Cheshire (2003) 'Pathways to work: Helping people into employment' consultation response. Leonard Cheshire

Lessof, C., Miller, M., Phillips, M., Pickering, K., Purdon, S. and Hales, J. (2003) *New Deal for Lone Parents Evaluation: Findings from the Quantitative Survey*, Research Report WAE 147, DWP

Levin-Epstein, J. (2003) 'Lifting the Lid Off the Family Cap' in *Childbearing and Reproductive Health Series*, Policy Brief 1, Center for Law and Social Policy

Lewis, J. (2003) 'Responsibilities and Rights: Changing the Balance' in Ellison, N. and Pierson, C. (eds.) *Developments in British Social Policy* 2 Palgrave Macmillan

Lewis, J. (1997) *Lone Mothers in European Welfare Regimes: Shifting Policy Logics,* Jessica Kingsley Publishers

Local Government Association (2003) *Response to the Anti-social Behaviour* White Paper LGA

Lodemel, I. (2004) 'The Development of Workfare within Social Activation Policies' in Gallie, D. (ed.) (2004) *Resisting Marginalization: Unemployment Experience and Social Policy in the European Union* Oxford University Press

Lodemel, I. and Trickey, H. (2001) *An Offer You Can't Refuse* Policy Press

London, A., Scott, E., Edin, K., and Hunter, V. (2004) 'Welfare Reform, Work-Family Trade-offs, and Child Well-being', in *Family Relations* 53 (2)

Loprest, P. (2003) *Fewer Welfare Leavers Employed in Weak Economy. Snapshots of America's Families III* No.5 The Urban Institute

Loumides, J., Stafford, B., Youngs, R., Green, A., Legard, R., Lessof, C., Lewis, J., Walker, R., Corden, A., Thornton, P. and Sainsbury, R. (2001) *Evaluation of the New Deal for Disabled People Personal Adviser Service Pilot* DWP

Marshall, T. (1950) 'Citizenship and Social Class', in *Citizenship and Social Class* Cambridge University Press

Mead, L. (1992) *The New Politics of Poverty: The Nonworking Poor in America* Basic Books

Mead, L. (ed.) (1997) *The New Paternalism* Brookings Institution

Mead, L. (2003) 'US Welfare Reform: The Institutional Dimension' in *Social Policy and Society* 2(2), Cambridge University Press

Mead, L. (2003a) 'Welfare Caseload Change: An Alternative Approach' in *Policy Studies Journal,* 31(2)

Mead, L. (2002) 'Rights and Responsibilities in American Social Policy' Paper prepared for presentation at ippr seminar available at www.ippr.org/research

Mill, J. (1985 [1859]) *On Liberty* Penguin

Millar, J. (2003) 'The Art of Persuasion? The British New Deal for Lone Parents' in Walker, R. and Wiseman, M. (2003) *The Welfare We Want?* US: International Specialized Book Services

Millar, J. and Evans, M. (2003) *Lone Parents and Employment: International Comparison of What Works* Centre for the Analysis of Social Policy

Miller, C. (2002) *Leavers, Stayers and Cyclers: An Analysis of the Welfare Caseload* MDRC

Ministry of Social Affairs and Health (2003) *Trends in Social Protection in Finland* available at www.stm.fi

Moffitt, R., Burton, L., and King, M. (2002) 'The Characteristics of Families Remaining on Welfare' in *Welfare, Children and Families Study* Policy Brief 02–2, Johns Hopkins University

Molloy, D. and Ritchie, J. (2000) *New Deal for Long-Term Unemployed People: Findings from a Qualitative Study Amongst Participants* DWP

Murray, C. (2001) 'Family Formation Issues in Welfare Reform' in Blank, R. and Haskins, R. (eds.) *The New World of Welfare*, Brookings Institution

Murray, C. (1984) *Losing Ground: American Social Policy, 1950-1980* Basic Books

National Centre for Social Research (2000) *British Social Attitudes Focusing on Diversity: The 17th Report* Sage Publications

Nelson, S. (2004) *Trends in Parents' Economic Hardship Snapshots of America's Families III No.21* The Urban Institute

Ochel, W. (2004) *Welfare-to-work Experiences with Specific Work-first Programmes in Selected Countries*, CESifo paper 1153 available at www.CESifo.de

OECD (2004) *OECD Economic Survey of the Netherlands 2004: Reform of the Sickness and Disability Benefit Schemes* OECD

OECD (2003) *Transforming Disability into Ability: Policies to Promote Work and Income Security for Disabled People* OECD

Pavetti, L. and Bloom, D. (2001) 'State Sanctions and Time Limits' in Blank, R. and Haskins, R. (eds.) *The New World of Welfare* Brookings Institution

Peter, M., Rousseau, N. and Lynam-Smith, C. (2003) *Evaluation of JSA literacy and numeracy pilots: final report* Research Report RR86 DfES

Pearce, D., Disney, J. and Ridout, H. (2002) *Making it Work, The Report of the Independent Review of Breaches and Penalties in the Social Security System* ACOSS

Phelps, L. and Wheatley, J. (2002) 'Anti-social legislation' in *Evidence* Citizens Advice

Piven, F. and Cloward, R (1993) *Regulating the Poor: The Functions of Public Welfare* 2nd edition, Vintage

Plant, R. (2003) 'Citizenship and Social Security' in *Fiscal Studies* 24(2):153–166

Populus (2004) 'The Times Poll' published in *The Times* 7 September

Rawls, J. (1999)[1971] *A Theory of Justice* Revised edition Harvard University Press

Rawls, J. (2001) *Justice as Fairness: A Restatement* Harvard University Press

Rector, R.E. (2001) 'The Effects of Welfare Reform' Available at www.heritage.org

Rector, R. and Youssef, S. (1999) *The Determinants of Welfare Caseload Decline* Heritage Foundation

Rupp, K. and Scott, C. (1998) 'Determinants of Duration on the Disability Rolls and Program Trends' in Rupp, K. and Stapleton, D. (eds.) *Growth in Disability Benefits: Explanations and Policy Implications* W.E. Upjohn Institute for Employment Research

Saunders, T., Stone, V. and Candy, S. (2001) *The Impact of the 26-week Sanctioning Regime* Research Report 100, Employment Service

Schmidt, L. and Sevak, P. (2002) *AFDC, SSI and Welfare Reform Aggressiveness: Caseload Reductions vs Caseload Shifting Working Paper* Williams College

Social Exclusion Unit (2000) *National Strategy for Neighbourhood Renewal – Report of Policy Action Team 7: Anti-Social Behaviour* ODPM

Social Security Online *Annual Statistical Report on the Social Security Disability Insurance Program 2002.* Available at www.ssa.gov

SSI (2002) *Statistical Annual Report 2002.* Available at www.ssa.gov

Stafford, B. (2003) 'Beyond Lone Parents: Extending Welfare-to-Work to Disabled People and the Young Unemployed' in Walker, R. and Wiseman, R. (eds.) *The Welfare We Want: The British challenge for American Reform* The Policy Press

Stanley, K. and Regan, S. (2003) *The Missing Million: Supporting Disabled People into Work* ippr

Stapleton, D. and Burkhauser, R. (eds) (2003) *The Decline in Employment of People with Disabilities* W.E. Upjohn Institute for Employment Research

Sunshine, J. and Tyler, T. (2003) 'The Role of Procedural Justice and Legitimacy in Shaping Public Support' in *Law and Society Review* 37(3) The Law and Society Association

Tawney, R. (1948) *The Acquisitive Society* Harcourt Brace

Thurley, D. (ed.) (2003) *Working to Target? Can Policies Deliver Paid Work for Seven in Ten Lone Parents?* One Parent Families

Urban Institute (2001) 'Jobs and Wages Up Sharply for Single Moms, Gains Especially High After Welfare Reform' in *Single Parents' Earnings Monitor* Urban Institute

Urban Institute (2002) *Fast Facts on Welfare Policy* Urban Institute

Urban Institute (2004) *Nearly 2 out of 5 Welfare Recipients Lack Knowledge of When Their Benefits End* Urban Institute

van Donselaar, G. (1998) *The Benefit of Another's Pains* University of Amsterdam

van Oorschot, W. (2004) 'Balancing Work and Welfare: Activation and Flexicurity in The Netherlands, 1980–2000' in *International Journal of Social Welfare* 13:15–27

van Oorschot, W. and Abrahamson, P. (2003) 'The Dutch and Danish Miracles Revisited: A Critical Discussion of Activation Policies in Two Small Welfare States' in *Social Policy and Administration* 37(3):288–304 Blackwell van Parijs, P. (1995) *Real Freedom for All: What (if Anything) can Justify Capitalism?* Oxford University Press

Vincent, J. (1998) *Jobseeker's Allowance Evaluation: Qualitative Research on Disallowed and Sanctioned Claimants* Research Report No 86, DFEE

Walker, R and Wiseman, M. (2003) 'Sharing ideas on Welfare?' in Walker, R. and Wiseman, M. (eds) (2003) *The Welfare We Want: The British Challenge for American Reform* The Policy Press

Weaver, R. (2000) *Ending Welfare as We Know It* Brookings Institution

Weil, A. (2002) *Ten Things Everyone Should Know About Welfare* Urban Institute

White, S. (2000) 'Social Rights and the Social Contract: Political Theory and the New Welfare Politics' in *British Journal of Political Science* 30:507–532

White, S. (2003) *The Civic Minimum: On the Rights and Obligations of Economic Citizenship* Oxford University Press

Williams, T., Hill, M. and Davies, R. (1999) *Attitudes to the Welfare State and the Response to Reform* DWP

Wittenburg, D. and Favreault, M. (2003) *Safety Net or Tangled Web?* New Federalism Occasional Paper No. 68, Urban Institute

Wittenburg, D. and Loprest, P. (2003) *A More Work Focused Disability Program? Challenges and Options* Urban Institute

Work Directions (2003) *Establishing a Framework for Vocational Rehabilitation* Ingeus Ltd

Zedlewski, S. (2002) *Left Behind or Staying Away? Eligible Parents who Remain Off TANF* Urban Institute

Zedlewski, S. (2003) *Work and Barriers to Work Among Welfare Recipients in 2002* Urban Institute

Zedlewski, S. and Alderson, D. (2001) *Beyond and After Reform: How Have Families on Welfare Changed?* Urban Institute

Zedlewski, S. and Loprest, P. (2001) 'Will TANF Work for the Most Disadvantaged Families?' in Blank, R. and Haskins, R. (eds.) *The New World of Welfare* Brookings Institution

Zedlewski, S., Giannarelli, L., Morton, J. and Wheaton, L. (2002) *Extreme Poverty Rising, Existing Government Programs Could Do More* Urban Institute

Zedlewski, S., Nelson, S., Edin, K., Koball, H., Pomper, K. and Roberts, T. (2003) *Families Coping without Earnings or Government Cash Assistance* Occasional Paper No.64 Urban Institute

Zilliak, J. (2003) 'Social Policy and the Macro-Economy: What Drives Welfare Caseloads in the US?' in *Social Policy and Society* 2(2):133–142 Cambridge University Press